Coaching Soccer

Robert "Butch" Lauffer

 Sterling Publishing Co., Inc.   New York

Edited by Timothy Nolan

Library of Congress Cataloging-in-Publication Data

Lauffer, Robert.
  Coaching soccer / by Robert "Butch" Lauffer.
    p.   cm.
  1. Soccer—Coaching.   2. Soccer for children—Coaching.
I. Title.
GV943.8.L38   1989
796.334'07'7—dc20   89-37639
                                               CIP

10 9 8 7 6 5 4 3

Copyright © 1989 by Robert A. Lauffer II
Published by Sterling Publishing Company, Inc.
387 Park Avenue South, New York, N.Y. 10016
Distributed in Canada by Sterling Publishing
% Canadian Manda Group, P.O. Box 920, Station U
Toronto, Ontario, Canada M8Z 5P9
Distributed in Great Britain and Europe by Cassell PLC
Villiers House, 41/47 Strand, London WC2N 5JE, England
Distributed in Australia by Capricorn Ltd.
P.O. Box 665, Lane Cove, NSW 2066
Manufactured in the United States of America
All rights reserved
Sterling ISBN 0-8069-6922-9 Trade
             0-8069-6923-7 Paper

Contents

Introduction

As a coach, I wrote this book for two reasons. The first was to say what I thought was the right way to develop soccer players. This can leave oneself open to criticism but also allows people to disagree, which should provoke intellectual thought about the game of soccer. This is desperately needed in this country.

The second reason was to identify and discuss the major philosophical coaching principles of the game, and tell how they can help the coaches, players, and the team collectively, as opposed to writing just another picture book (i.e., how to kick, dribble, etc.)

Coaches will also find practices to get these desired principles into his team's play, and a list of coaching points after each practice for the coach to identify, to see if his players are training correctly.

In the end I hope the coach will find the book easy to read and follow, as well as stimulating enough to open one's eyes even further about the game of soccer.

It would be impossible to list all the events and people that have affected my coaching philosophy. Being American I was very fortunate to gain international experience and exposure at a relatively young age. This, in part, is why I wrote this book. However, I never imagined it would turn out to be a five year project. Therefore, I would like to dedicate this book to the people who helped make it a reality. First I would like to mention and thank Ron Griffith and the Texas Longhorn Soccer Club, who provided me with the opportunity to see both the world in general and the soccer world; this hopefully has made me a better coach by expanding my horizons on how the game should be played. The second person I would like to mention is John Riley, who I have had the great pleasure to play under and to work with, and who unknowingly inspired me to finish this book. The third person I would like to thank is David Baker for putting up with my late night discussions and trying to decipher my drawings on pizza boxes. A big thank you goes to Steve Wolf for his continuous advisement—without his perseverance this book would probably not be a reality. Last but not least I would like to thank my parents, Robert and Ann Lauffer, for putting up with my soccer adventures, and for providing me with all the love, support, and guidance that any son could ask for.

About the Author

Robert "Butch" Lauffer has been playing soccer since the age of seven, and today is one of a new generation of young soccer coaches who grew up playing the game in the United States and abroad.

Starting with the North Texas State Soccer Association under-19 state team in 1979, Butch went on to play with the famed Texas Longhorn Soccer Club in Dallas. He played in over 100 games for the club, traveling to Mexico, England, Scotland, Wales, Northern Ireland, Finland, West Germany, Austria, Norway, Luxembourg, Italy, France, Sweden, and Denmark, in addition to tournaments such as the Gothia Cup (twice), the Helsinki Cup, and the Munich Cup. In 1980 the Longhorns won the Munich Cup, a tremendous upset, as this was the first United States team to win a major European tournament. Later he trained and traveled with the Longhorns' under-12, under-14, and under-16 teams to England and Scotland—all by the age of 20.

Butch attended the Carnegie School of Physical Education and Human Movement in Leeds, England, from 1981 to 1983, where he played soccer and earned Player of the Year honors in 1983. He returned to the United States and received his Bachelor's Degree in kinesiology in 1984 from Texas Christian University, where he was also captain of the soccer team. He received his Master's Degree from T.C.U. in 1988.

From 1984 to 1986, Butch worked with the North Texas State Soccer Association in training and picking players for the state team, as well as conducting licensing courses for coaches. He was a staff coach for the United States Youth Soccer Federation in 1987, and a national team administrator for the tours of Scotland and Las Cruces in 1988 and the Granatkin Tournament in Russia in 1989.

His coaching education includes the English Football Association preparatory course and preliminary badge and the United States Soccer Federation "A" License. He also just recently received the Irish Football Association Grade One coaching license, making him one of the very few American coaches to hold a full license from a foreign country.

Presently Mr. Lauffer is the coaching director of the Spring Soccer Club, in Spring, Texas, which has a youth enrollment of over one thousand players.

Acknowledgements

Sally Armstrong—Editing/Typing, TCU, Ft. Worth, Texas
Jackie Hodges—Editing/Typing, TCU, Ft. Worth, Texas
Linda Kay—Photographs, Ft. Worth, Texas
Ed Lawrence—Photographs, Kingwood, Texas
Dana Adams—Illustrations, Tyler, Texas
Paula Wells—Illustrations, Kingwood, Texas
Texas Longhorns '72—Players
Ft. Worth United '71—Players
Robin Sanders—Photo Organization
Eric Davis—Fitness Consultant

1   Technique and Skill

What is the difference between technique and skill, and how can a coach take a technically sound player and make him or her a highly successful one?

Illus. 1

Illus. 2

Illus. 1 and Illus. 2. Technique is a sound pattern of body movement within a given sport. Skill, however, is the learned ability to use these techniques to advantage during the conditions and restrictions of a game. My favorite definition of skill comes from Barbara Knapp: "Skill is a learned ability to bring about predetermined results with maximum certainty, often with the minimum outlay of time and energy or both." In other words, the

one who expends the least amount of energy for the same results will have the advantage and therefore will be more skillful. An example of this skill would be the gracefulness of Franz Beckenbauer or Johan Cruyff, both of whom played soccer at the highest level seemingly effortlessly.

Before any player can be highly skilled he must be technically sound. There are three stages to teaching technique: the fundamental stage, the game-related stage and the match-related stage.

Fundamental Stage

Previously, teaching soccer fundamentals was a stationary practice. Two standing players would pass the ball back and forth, or one would hand-serve the ball and the other would head it back to him. These days this concept is obsolete.

One player still hand-serves to his partner who volleys the ball back to him. But this time, he varies the service from high to low to medium range, as well as short or out to the side of the working player. This makes the working player move while performing the technique.

Illus. 3. In a game situation a perfect ball to volley rarely occurs; the player almost always makes some type of adjustment to the flight of the ball, so why not train players for this in practice, so they can handle the situation in the game? The player does not have the pressure of opponents, time, and space; however, internal pressure to improve is built into the practice.

Illus. 4

Illus. 4. Incorporate movement into every practice for fundamental training, even with under-8 players. Having these youngsters dribble through cones is a waste of time, and here's why: Let's say you have two lines of seven with the cones five yards apart in front of them. In this organization you will have two players working (dribbling) and twelve players standing in line—pulling hair, throwing dirt, and everything else imaginable to a seven-year-old. This is inefficient in terms of the amount of time each player has working with the ball. Get *all* your players working at the same time.

When practising any technique, make sure the player's service is good—poor service causes many interruptions and lends no fluidity to the practice. The players spend more time chasing balls than working on desired techniques.

Make adjustments to service. Change from a foot to a hand service, or move the players if they are not working together.

Game-Related Stage

Illus. 5. This stage introduces the concepts of opponent pressure and time and space restrictions. Instead of expecting your players to work under full game pressure all at once, introduce the elements gradually.

With these multiple pressures, the working player must speed up his technical movements. He must improve his ability to bring

Illus. 5

the ball under control quickly as well as speed up his decision-making: to turn away from the opponent, pass, or shoot on goal.

If players are not achieving success, reduce or expand the time, space and opponent restrictions.

Match Condition Stage

Illus. 6

Illus. 6. In this stage, players perform techniques under full match conditions. This training requires the continuous pressure of time, space and opponents which occurs in the actual match. As the player's skill increases, time and space conditions should become more restricted and more opponents added.

Functional Training

Functional training is specialized towards particular position; goalkeepers, fullbacks, midfielders and strikers.

Stay alert to the emotional needs of your players. Many times the coach will go to practice with a plan, but if a player is not having success, be prepared to digress or move on. Simplify the technical practice in order to achieve success.

II Strategy, Tactics, and Systems of Play

Teaching Tactics

Just as coaching techniques have a series of steps leading to the implementation of techniques under game conditions, so also does the coaching of tactics follow a progressive buildup pattern. Tactics fall into three categories: individual, group, and team.

Strategy is the planning of a long-term goal—for example, planning to win a league championship or a state cup championship. Tactics are the plans you make in order to win a particular game. By observing the opponent's style of play, you can adjust your team's tactics. For instance, if you notice that the other team plays without a sweeper, your team can practise playing balls over the top of the fullbacks and letting the strikers run on to them.

Tactics do not apply only to attacking, but to defensive soccer as well. Let's say that a team is playing against one that likes to play balls over the top and run after them. As a defensive tactic, strikers and midfielders can apply pressure and shut down on the long service from fullbacks and midfielders.

Individual Tactics

Individual tactics refer to one-on-one confrontations between players. This is fundamental to handling any kind of tactic.

Illus. 7

Illus. 7. The first tactical consideration is maintaining possession of the ball. Teach the player to shield the ball from his opponent to help maintain possession.

The next tactical consideration is the concept of time and space. Learning how to create time and space in the one-on-one situation is vital. If the attacking player can create the time and space he needs, he can beat his opponent by the dribble, the pass or the shot on goal. If the attacking player is without the ball, he can win it back through the tackle.

Illus. 8. On defense, the player must win possession of the ball as early as possible. He must also deny the attacking player time and space. If the defender is unable to achieve these two, he must then prevent the attacking player from making any penetration through a dribble or a shot on the goal. If the attacking player is not in possession of the ball, the defending player, through good, tight marking, prevents him from receiving the ball.

Possession of the ball is won and lost by individual players, and the more refined the tactics of the individuals, the longer and more frequent will be the team's possession of the ball.

Group Tactics

Illus. 9. Maintaining possession of the ball is the main principle of soccer, and one of the best ways to maintain possession is to have numerical superiority over the opposition. This necessitates players working in groups to provide cover in defense and support in attack. The more defenders a team has in the

Illus. 8

area of the ball, the greater is its chance of winning possession. The more attackers there are in the area of the ball, the greater the number of passing opportunities, which increases the probability of maintaining possession of the ball.

Illus. 10. Group tactics refers to the number organization starting at two-on-one through five-on-five. At no time are all 11 players involved equally. Each player must be able to handle the small games (the two-on-one or three-on-two situations, et cetera) within the large game. Thus, most tactical training will be done at this stage.

Teaching tactics at the group stage teaches players to solve problems that occur during a match. By adding more attacking and defending players, the problems become more complex, and making the right decision at the

Illus. 9

Illus. 10

right time becomes even harder. For these tactics to be most realistic, have the players perform in the restricted space directly proportional to the number of players involved.

Team Tactics: Six-on-Four to Eleven-on-Eleven

When teaching team tactics the coach must concentrate on individual play as well as combination play. He must teach his players responsibility in attacking and defending all three parts of the field (attack, midfield, defense).

Team tactics also include all restart situations, such as kick-offs, free kicks, throw-ins, penalty kicks and corner kicks. The final stage is teaching the team the skill of successful counter-attacking.

Tactical Practices

There are three stages to teaching tactics:

keeping possession, going to one goal, and adding a counter-attack goal.

Start with one-on-one in a 10 yard by 10 yard grid, having the two players try to maintain possession. Add a central goal, having them attack and defend one goal; then add the counter-attack goal. This will complete the transition from attack to defense, which all players will have to do in the game.

Divide the tactical implications into two areas, attack and defense, and organize the drills as follows:

Attack *(Illus. 11)*
Shielding the ball
Creating time and space
Beating a player by the dribble

Defense
Tackle
Denying time and space
Jockeying

Illus. 11

Adding One Goal *(Illus. 12)*

Attack

Shielding
Creating time and space
Beating players by the dribble
Beating players by shooting

Defense

Tackle
Denying time and space
Jockeying
Defending against the shot

Illus. 12

Illus. 13

Add Counter-Attack Goal *(Illus. 13)*

Attack

Shielding
Creating time and space
Beating players by the dribble
Beating players by shooting
Transition from attack to defense

Defense

Tackle
Denying time and space
Jockeying
Defending against the shot on goal
Transition from defense to attack

The Use of Restrictions

Using restrictions in practice is a great way to emphasize particular elements. However, do not add restrictions for their own sake. Some good examples of restrictions are: one touch; two touch; certain number of passes before a shot on goal can be taken; certain number of wall passes, take-overs, or short-short-long passes. Restricting short-short-long passes develops the players' ability to switch the play or point of attack.

Systems of Play

Illus. 14–15. In the soccer world, systems of play tend to change every four years, right after the World Cup. Brazil, for instance, won its first title with its 4-2-4 formation at the 1958 World Cup, and England won its only World Cup in 1966 with Alf Ramsey's 4-4-2 formation. Because of these teams' successes, other national and club teams began copying these formations. Even though both these sytems were built around the strengths and weaknesses of the players on those teams. The players dictated the type of system used. For example, Alf Ramsey felt that there were no world-class wingers available to him. Be-

Illus. 14

cause of this, England used four players in midfield and relied on their outside midfielders and fullbacks to overlap into attacking positions.

Because of the pressure to win, coaches are willing to copy other teams' successful systems, even if it's inappropriate for their personnel. Because of these fads, certain types of players and elements of the game are sometimes abandoned. As a result of England's World Cup victory with its four midfielders, out-and-out wingers disappeared from the English League, as well as from the international game. Now, twenty years later, wingers are reappearing on the field.

Illus. 15

III Warm-Ups and Conditioning

A proper warm-up allows players to run faster, jump higher, and kick farther. It also reduces the chance of injury as well as preparing the player mentally for competition—it "gets his head in the game."

It is the coach's job to convince his players of the benefits of a warm-up. Remember that the mind controls the body. A well-trained athlete may require fifteen to thirty minutes to warm up, but a less trained or less experienced player warming up for this long may become more physically fatigued and even rebellious towards the coach, the practice, or the game itself.

Physically, a proper warm-up raises the body temperature, which in turn increases muscle elasticity and flexibility, thus reducing the possibility of soreness and muscle tearing. Oxygen intake and breathing efficiency are also increased. Mentally, a good warm-up activates the memory needed for specific movements that will be necessary during the game. A player is properly warmed up when he is sweating freely. This usually indicates about a 2° rise in body temperature.

Coaches should use both the *general warm-up*, which includes jogging, stretching, and other body preparation exercises, and the *specific warm-up*, which are techniques that will be used in games as well as exercises to build endurance, speed, and strength.

The General Warm-Up

Jogging Exercises

Illus. 16. Hold the hands waist high in front and lift knees to hands while jogging.

Illus. 16

Illus. 17. Hold hands behind and lift heels to hands while jogging.

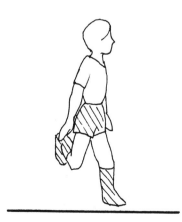

Illus. 17

Illus. 18. Jump and head at an imaginary ball while jogging (both one- and two-footed takeoffs).

Illus. 18

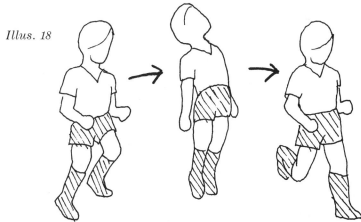

Illus. 19. Turn sideways and shuffle-step side-to-side.

Illus. 19

Illus. 20

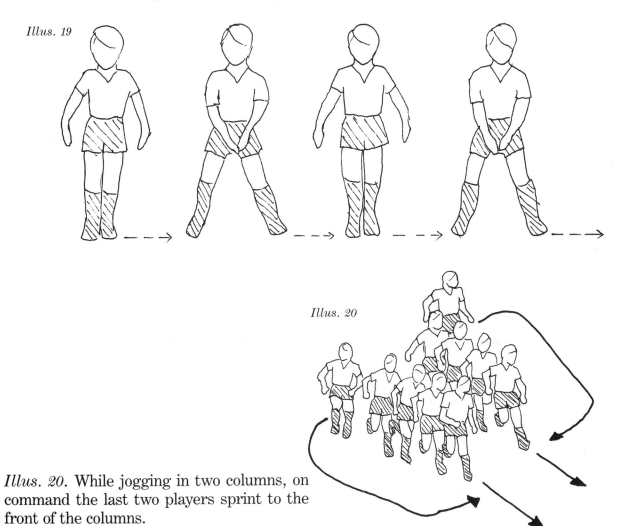

Illus. 20. While jogging in two columns, on command the last two players sprint to the front of the columns.

Ball Exercises

Illus. 21. With feet together, jump forward and backwards over the ball.

Illus. 22. With feet together, jump from side to side over the ball.

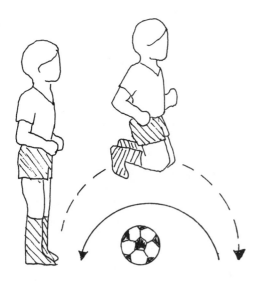

Illus. 21

Illus. 22

Illus. 23. While standing, throw the ball into the air, then sit down, get back up and catch or control the ball before it hits the ground.

Illus. 23

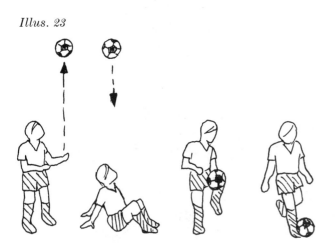

Illus. 24. While standing, throw the ball into the air, do a forward roll, then catch or control the ball before it hits the ground.

Illus. 24

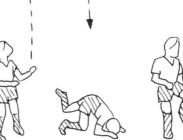

20

Stretching

Having players stretch only at the beginning of a warm-up is asking for injury. A muscle is like a rubber band—it stretches much better warm than cold, and breaks easier cold than warm.

In addition, stretching exercises not only elongate the muscle fibres, but the tissue connecting these fibres as well—the tendons and the ligaments. Therefore, through proper stretching, there will be improved mobility, as well as properly relaxed muscles.

The best way to achieve this is through the static stretch. This is a slow stretch to the point of feeling the muscle pull. Stop and repeat the process. Remember, though, never to bounce while performing a stretch, because a cold or warm muscle can tear!

Illus. 26. Hamstring stretch

Illus. 25. Quadricep stretch

Illus. 27. Groin stretch using a side-to-side butterfly

Illus. 28. Calf stretch

Illus. 29. V-stretch

22

Some soccer players have very tight muscles, making it difficult to stretch. To help these players, use a partner stretch with proprioceptive neuromuscular foscilitation (PNF). Stretch the muscle group until tension is felt. Hold for ten seconds; then push against the partner with the partner providing isometric resistance. Hold for five seconds. After this five-second contraction the partner will again stretch this muscle group until tension is felt. After 3 or 4 repetitions an increase in flexibility will be seen.

Illus. 30. An example of PNF stretching is stretching the hamstring. To stretch the hamstrings, the player lifts the leg with the knee locked out until he feels tension in the hamstrings. The partner holds the leg locked as well as applying the isometric pressure to keep the leg in place. The player then pushes down with maximal effort, keeping the knee extended, for the last five seconds. When the player relaxes the partner should carefully push the leg farther when the procedure is repeated. Repeat several times.

Illus. 30

The Specific Warm-Up

Ball Exercises

Illus. 31. Dribble the ball throughout the field, remembering to change pace.

Illus. 32–33. Juggle the ball, remembering the height of the juggle.

Illus. 33

Illus. 34. Drive and chip long, interpassing with two, three, or four players, always moving.

Illus. 35. Use a five-on-two playing in a floating grid or a marked grid, with the five players keeping away from the two.

Always try to incorporate the soccer ball in a specific warm-up, as well as involving technical work. Remember: most coaches only get their teams twice a week for training, so all the ball work that can be worked in helps.

Always try to make the specific warm-up as realistic as possible. Most of your players will respond better to exercises with the ball, if for no other reason than that it's more fun.

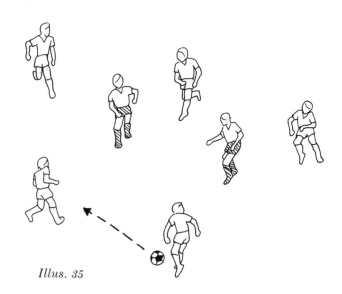

Illus. 35

Practice:

Illus. 36–38. Have the server serve the ball underhand to the other player either seven, ten, or twelve yards away. He then brings the ball back to the server, returning to the starting spot, performing the specific drill.

Illus. 36

Illus. 36. Use a first-time volley or half-volley.

Illus. 37

Illus. 37. Use a first-time header.

Illus. 38

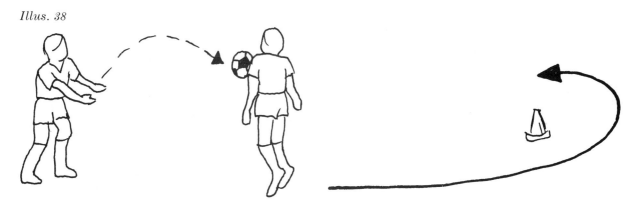

Illus. 38. Control with the chest; then volley the ball back.

Game-day warm-ups should prepare your players in mind and body for their best performance. Combine both general and specific warm-up techniques, and keep changing them, so they don't get stale. Also, use this as a cooling-down after practices or games.

Cooling down becomes especially important in tournament play, when you may only have two to three hours between games and are looking to prevent soreness. Cooling down accelerates the reduction of lactic acid levels in blood and muscle, as well as keeping muscles contracting, which helps prevent blood from pooling in the extremities.

Endurance

Endurance delays fatigue, sustains activity longer and enhances recovery. Lack of endurance results in diminished performance due to poor concentration, timing and muscle coordination. Developing your players' endurance is a must. There are two types of endurance: general and local.

General, or cardiovascular endurance, enables a player to sustain activity in many large muscles and thus withstand the intensity of a full match. The muscles must have oxygen brought to them through the circulatory system, thus practising general endurance makes sure that the body has plenty of oxygen which will supply the working muscles. This foundation must be laid first before the coach can take his players further in developing fitness.

Practice:

The best way to develop oxygen supply to the muscle is interval training. In interval training players perform short spans of hard work with brief recovery periods. The objective is to perform a maximum amount of work before fatigue sets in. The principle dictates work at a pulse rate of about 180 beats per minute for one to three minutes. The rest should be done at a pulse rate of about 120 beats per minute for one to one and a half minutes; then repeat the cycle.

Illus 39. The players sprint the length of the field, 120 yards, within sixteen seconds. In their rest interval, they jog back to the starting line within one minute. Repeat, but never exceed ten repetitions.

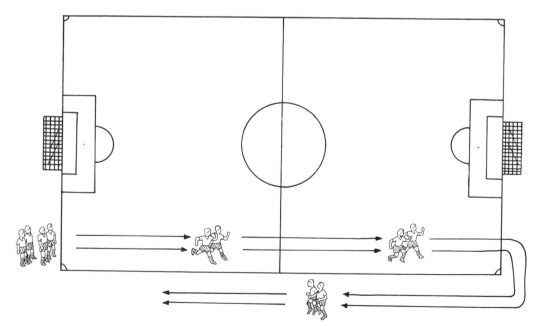

Illus. 39

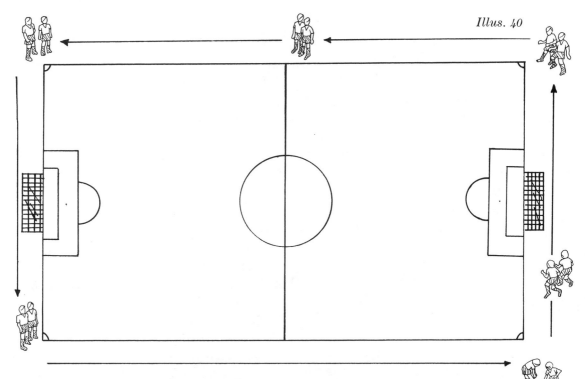

Illus. 40. Relay race around the field. Three to one work ratio.

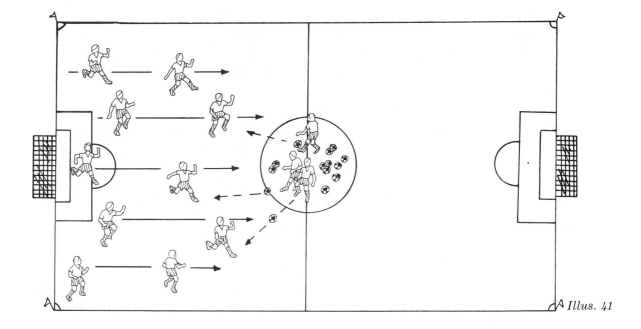

Illus. 41

Illus. 41. The Hunted Game. The coach picks two or three players and puts them in mid-field. The rest of the team is at one end of the touch line. At the command the players at the touch line sprint from one end to the other without getting hit with a ball. When a player is hit he joins the hunters until the end.

Local endurance, asking a localized muscle group to repeat or sustain many contractions, requires a greater energy source than the aerobic process can supply. The breakdown of glycogen to lactic acid can make energy available. This is called the *anaerobic* process, and is sometimes referred to as working under oxygen debt. The lactic acid which then builds up in the muscle is a fatigue toxic. When the muscle can no longer stand the level of lactic acid, it will slow down or stop working.

Practice:

A widely used and popular exercise with coaches, but not with players, is shuttle running. Mark off an area 25 yards long in five-yard sections. The players sprint to the first marker; then back to the starting line; then to the next marker; then back to the starting line, and so on until finished. This exercise should not last longer than 40 seconds with older players. Rest and repeat. Shuttle running also duplicates the type of running done in the match with quick starts, stops and turns.

It is obvious that general and local endurance are closely related, and many exercises can be used to develop both. When selecting an exercise for endurance training, remember that lactic acid is produced during the anaerobic state after 35 seconds of work. Be careful not to take your players over the limit.

Pressure Training

Pressure training involves use of the ball and is therefore entertaining as well as economical. It is also helpful in developing both a local and general endurance.

In pressure training, one player is served soccer balls continuously for thirty to sixty seconds. He must return them to the coach or direct them to some target (the goal) using a soccer technique. To increase the pressure, the coach need only to increase the time factor and/or the frequency of the balls.

Practice:

Illus. 42–44. Groups of two, one ball, one cone. One player will serve the ball using an underhand serve to the working player, who will play the ball back to the server. After playing the ball back he must turn and sprint around the cone and repeat. Position the serving player 20 yards from the cone.

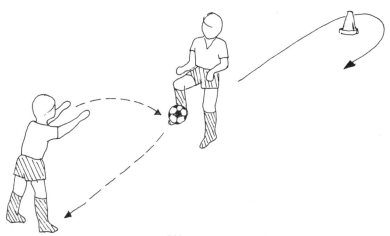

Illus. 42. First time volleys

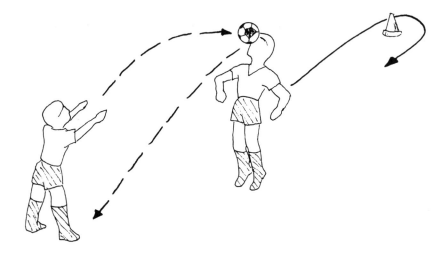

Illus. 43. First time heading

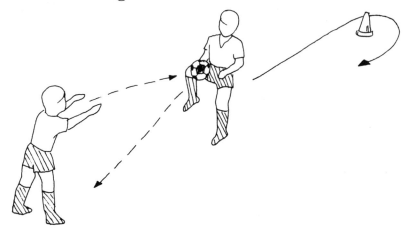

Illus. 44. Control and pass back

Illus 45. Use groups of three with one ball. The working player will receive the pass, collect, turn, and pass to the next player who will pass it back to the working player. Repeat. Have the two end players stand 20 to 25 yards apart.

Speed

Speed is a very complex idea. Running fast from point A to point B does not make someone a great soccer player, and a player can be a slow runner but a fast player. Pure speed is the ability to run a measured distance in a measured time; for example, a 40-yard dash. Many elements of practice can help a player in this way, but pure speed is an innate ability. A person can improve his or her pure speed 12 to 15%, but that's all. It is a God-given talent that will never greatly improve—one cannot put in what God left out.

Pure Speed Practice

Have the players perform a slow high knee exercise over a five-yard and a ten-yard distance. During the practice, have the players concentrate on form: knees high, elbows bent and close to the body, and head still. The player also wants to count how many steps he can perform while he is in a designated area; the higher the better.

Next, have the players sprint at 50% over the designated distance—20 yards, 30 yards, 40 yards, 50 yards. During this exercise the player should concentrate on form.

Next, have the player sprint 75 to 80% of his full speed over the same designated area, and finish by having them sprint at full speed over the same area. Remember to start low on your distance and high on repetitions; then build up.

Ball Speed Practice

The amount of time and space that a player has, as well as the tempo of the game, is determined by a player's ball speed or technical speed—how fast a player can bring the ball under control and do something positive with it, such as dribble away, pass, or shoot. All the technique practice that the player can do under pressure of time, space, and opponents will help him become a technically faster player.

Illus. 46. Have a six-on-four keep away game, but when one of the six players has possession

Illus. 46

of the ball, that player must touch the ball with his feet a predetermined number of times. For example, if that number is three, the player may receive the ball off his chest, get the ball to the ground and touch the ball three times as fast as he can; then pass it off to a supporting teammate and so on.

Illus. 47. To work on quick acceleration, have every player handle the ball and dribble at a moderate pace. Push the ball ten yards forward; then on command from the coach, the player sprints forward to catch it. Repeat.

Illus. 48. Two players face each other in pairs three to four yards apart. The player with the ball pushes it through his partner's legs. The partner must then turn and sprint to catch it. Reverse and repeat.

Illus. 47

Illus. 48

Hill Work Practice

Hill work is a great way to enhance speed.

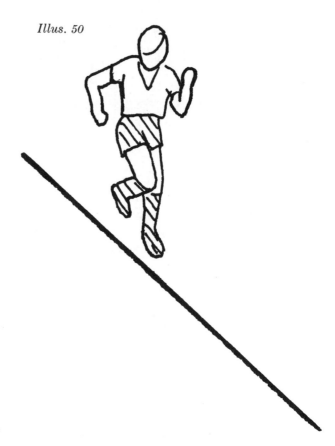

Illus. 49

Illus. 49. Running uphill develops a player's leg drive and increases quadricep (thigh) and gastrocnemius (calf) muscles. This helps in muscle coordination, which helps develop overall power.

Illus. 50. Running downhill helps the athlete's mechanics—his rate of striding and stride length.

Illus. 51

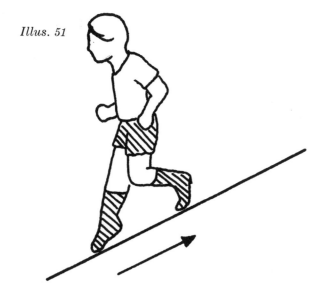

Illus. 51. Running uphill backwards will help muscle balance between the quads and the hamstrings, thus reducing chance of muscle pulls.

Illus. 52

Tactical speed

Illus. 52. Tactical speed refers to the player's ability to "read the game" and make the best decision rapidly. The players learn this through both experience and trial and error, but must be coached in tactics to understand the game and to anticipate the play of opponents.

Remember that running is an integral part of the game of soccer. Try not to use running as a form of punishment. You don't want to turn your players against running, or the game.

Strength

Strength is probably the single most important factor in athletic performance. It helps develop speed and quickness, and reduces the chance of injury.

Strength is the ability of the body (or part of the body) to apply force. Since the application of force at a rapid rate results in power, strength development is important for any team player. Unfortunately, though, strength development and weight training usually conjure up ideas of muscle-bound individuals with little mobility. But for the soccer player, strength and power are very important, whether kicking a long ball, shooting on goal, changing direction, or accelerating down the field. Strength is needed even to face differences in field and weather conditions. Thus, it is well worth the coaches' time to work on strength development.

A simple method for developing strength is

repetition of technique. Kicking, shooting, and heading all require strength. Exercising these skills will improve muscle coordination and increase strength through repeated muscle contraction and application of a resistance force (the ball). Repetition of technique may be boring, but there is no other way for the player to develop these specific strength and coordination skills.

Another way for a soccer player to develop strength is through weight training, specifically the "overload" principle. This allows the player to contract muscles regularly against greater-than-normal resistance. The resistance must be increased as muscle strength increases. Keep in mind, though, that as a rule weight training is most beneficial in the off-season, and should only be used to maintain strength during the season.

Increase the number of sets performed in each exercise and their proximity to maximum effort depend on the individual's inititial fitness, and on his progress. After approximately six weeks in the program, the athlete should be doing three sets of six to ten repetitions of each exercise. The first two sets should ease the muscles progressively into the third set, which should be done at near maximum effort.

Weight training is the best way to increase strength in one's players, but the use of weights for young players should not start until the age of fourteen or fifteen. This is because the muscles, ligaments and skeletal structure in the body are not stable enough in younger players and may be easily damaged. Technique repetition, plus simple push-ups and sit-ups, is the better way to build strength in young players.

Thirty seconds to one minute of jogging followed by three to five minutes of walking is a good cool-down. This will allow the body to effect the necessary readjustments.

Preparing a Weight Training Program:
• Select weights for each exercise that the player can lift 8–10 times by 3 sets.
• Perform the workout three times per week.
• Perform the full range of motion during each exercise.
• Increase weight progressively at an average rate of 5% each week to maintain the overload principle.
• Maintain proper breathing during all weight training exercise, inhaling before exertion and exhaling during exertion.

Weight Examples

Illus. 53. Bench press.

Illus. 54

Illus. 54–55. Military press

Illus. 55

Illus. 56–58. Squats

Illus. 56

Illus. 57

Illus. 58

38

Illus. 59. Knee extension

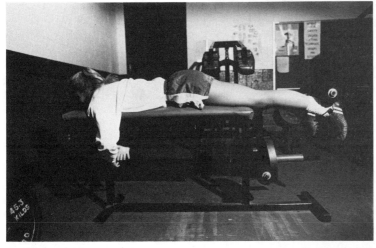

Illus. 60

Illus. 60–61. Hamstring extension

Illus. 61

Illus. 62

Illus. 62–63. Sit-ups

Illus. 63

IV   Defense

The primary objective of defense is to deny an opponent goal-scoring opportunities. Within this larger challenge there are defensive principles which will help any defending team succeed in denying goals. These principles are: time and space, pressuring, marking, support and depth, concentration and balance.

Time and Space

Illus. 64. Time and space are the two intangibles that work in soccer. The attacker wants more space, which allows him more time on the ball, more time for technical decisions, and more room for error. The defending player tries to minimize the space available to the attacker, cutting down on his time with the ball and his decision-making ability. Thus, limiting the opponent's time and space will automatically increase his errors.

Illus. 64

Pressuring

Illus. 65

is applied properly, the player with the ball does not have time to assess the situation and make the best decision.

Communication is very important. The supporting defending players should pass on verbal information to help the player who is pressuring the ball. This should guide the pressuring player; for example, hold, push, or shadow the attacking player in one direction or another. Teammates may instruct the pressuring player to push the attacking player towards the touch line, or to more supporting defenders. The supporting defender has to be the pressuring player's eyes.

When pressure is applied to attacking players, it makes them put their heads down. Three things can result without giving up a goal: the defending player can intercept the opposition passes; the defending player can challenge for the ball and win it through a successful tackle; or the defending player can pressure the attacker and force him to lose the ball out of play.

Illus. 65. Defenders must pressure attacking players whenever possible, especially the one in possession, in order to force mental or technical mistakes. This high pressure tactic can be very successful when playing teams that are not skilled on the ball. It can also break up the rhythm of your opponent, especially with a team that likes to build from the back.

Illus. 66. A common fault occurs when a defensive player applies pressure to the man on the ball but his teammates do not close down the attacking player, supporting players, and the passing lanes. When this happens, the player applying the pressure will waste his energy, and his teammates will allow him to be taken out of the game. When the pressure

Illus. 66

Practice:

Have a one-on-one play in a 10-yard by 20-yard grid. Have the two players each trying to get to each other's end line; then move the practice to add more players; two-on-two, three-on-three, and so on, playing in the proper grid size. Start with keeping possession and then add goals *(Illus. 67)*.

Illus. 67

Playing small-sided games allows for more frequent practise in pressuring opponents and giving verbal communication in match play situations *(Illus. 68)*.

Illus. 68

• *Deny time and space*. Denying space to the opponent will also limit his time to play. When his time is limited he must be better technically as well as mentally. Everything is speeded up.

• *Avoid diving in*. If the pressuring player dives in and is beaten, the whole supporting role of his teammates will collapse, because one of the supporting players will have to leave the player he was marking to pressure the attacker with the ball.

• *Close down as a unit*. Too many times the pressuring player will close down quickly, but his supporting players will not. This leaves the attacking player with passing options to get him out of trouble.

Illus. 69

Illus. 70

• *Judge distance*. If the pressuring players are not the proper distance from the attacking players with the ball, the attacking players have time to get their heads up and view the field. By being too far from the opponent, players leave the passing lanes open. If the distance is too small, the defending player may be beaten by the dribble *(Illus. 69–70)*.

• *Communication*. Verbal communication is necessary for good defense. Provide the pressuring player with verbal support so he has direction. In most cases the supporting defending player does the directing.

• *Proper stance*. Remember to coach the players in the proper defensive stance. Defending players often come out to meet attacking players and stand square to them. When this happens, the attacking players can push the ball by them on either side and the attacker can beat the defender by playing the ball through the opponent's legs, or "nutmegging" him. If the defending players stand with one foot in front of the other, like fencers, they can react to the attacking players movements more easily.

• *Use of the field*. When pressuring opponents there are parts of the field that are more advantageous than others. If you try to pressure opponents in corners of the field, you limit their space because of the two touch lines. However, if you try to pressure players in the middle of the field, they have the whole field to get out of trouble. Use the field to your advantage. Applying pressure in the wrong parts of the field at the wrong times, will punish your players *(Illus. 71)*.

Illus. 71

Marking Players

In youth soccer, one area that coaches often neglect is defensive marking, from normal play to set pieces. With emphasis on attacking soccer and skill training, it's easy to forget the skill and intelligence required for good defending.

It sounds simple, but if a team can keep the other team from scoring, it only needs to score one goal to win. The higher the level a team achieves, the fewer chances it will have to score. At a high level, one marking mistake will mean the game.

Illus. 72. When standing on the sidelines, one will always hear the battle cry "goal side!" The term refers to the defending players and the goal.

Illus. 73

Illus. 73. Here, the back four players are marking goal side. This is not good enough. By marking just goal side the attacking midfield player can still play the ball into his teammate's feet. To discourage this, your defending players must also mark ball side as well. Marking this way will discourage any type of passes to those players at all, and if the player on the ball does try to pass, the defender can intercept the pass and initiate the counterattack. However, the defending player must not over-commit and get turned by the attacker.

Practice:

(Two-on-one, two-on-two, three-on-three)

Illus. 74

Illus. 74. Use small-sided games, and start with two-on-one: Two attacking players; one server, one receiver and one defender. The server plays the ball to the receiver, who is being marked. The marking player works both goal side and ball side. Have the server pass from different angles, making the defender readjust his marking position. Build up the practice by adding more players in the proper grid size, keeping possession and adding goals.

As previously mentioned, avoid getting caught standing square. The defending team does not want to get caught square on their last line of defense in a straight line. You want depth in your defense. One penetrating pass can take numerous players out of the game.

Keep numbers up around the ball. The defending team always wants to have a numbers-up situation. In other words, have more defenders around the ball than attacking players.

Finally, avoid marking the least dangerous man too tightly. Usually the least dangerous man is the man farthest from the ball during attack. Marking this player too tightly can throw the depth factor out of balance and make the defense flat.

• *Proper marking distance.* One of the keys to proper marking is learning the distance at which the defending player should mark the attacking player. Unfortunately, the only way to really learn this is through trial and error, and by learning opponents' strengths and weaknesses, as well as their own.

• *Getting goal side.* Keep the defensive player running between the attacking player he is marking and the goal.

• *Getting ball side.* The defending player wants to position himself goal side of the attacking player as well as ball side. By doing this he discourages any passes to the attacking player's feet.

• *Making the interception.* When the defending player marks goal and ball side he is now in the position to make the interception and start the counterattack.

• *Make the tackle.* If the defending player is unable to make the interception, he must be prepared to make the tackle.

• *Avoiding being turned.* The defending player must not over-commit and get turned by the attacking player.

Support/Depth

Attacking players need support to provide options and maintain possession of the ball. Defenders need support to minimize the penetration of players and balls. In defense as in attack, a triangle formation provides adequate support and depth. Support and depth are necessary to not only restrict space into which the attacker's passes and the attackers themselves can travel, but to provide cover for defenders and for dangerous space, which attacking players could exploit.

Illus. 75. The most visible example of support on the soccer field is the depth which the sweeper provides for the fullbacks.

Illus. 75

Illus. 76. The job of the sweeper is to provide cover for the fullbacks who are marking the opposing strikers. If the sweeper gets caught too square, the whole back line can be beaten with one penetrating pass, dribble, or run.

Illus. 77. Usually, the back four players provide the depth, but one of the most common breakdowns in this concept occurs when the point of attack is on one side of the field and the opposite side fullback does not come around and provide support and depth in defense. By failing to do this, he leaves open the option of the attacking team exploiting the space behind the defense.

SPACE TO BE EXPLOITED

Illus. 77

Illus. 78. In this example, the sweeper has gone to provide support and depth to the right back. This pulls the sweeper out of the middle of the field and opens up space behind the defense. To prevent this, the left back must slide over and become the extra sweeper. If the left back is marking a player, he needs to drop deep enough so that he can see the ball and the player he is marking at the same time. Too many times, the back will fall into the trap of pushing over too far and still let the man get in behind him.

This concept of defensive support goes on all over the field, from the simplest form of one-on-two to the largest form of eleven-on-eleven.

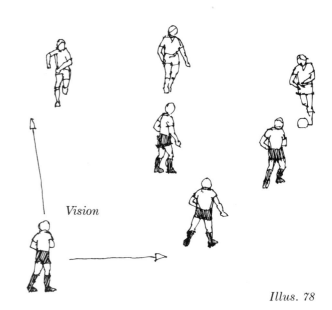

Vision

Illus. 78

Practice:

Introduce the supporting element by having one-on-two; one attacking player against two defenders in a 15-yard wide by 20-yard long grid. The attacking player tries to score a goal by getting to the touch line.

Illus. 79. Defender number 2 is providing support for defender number 1. Remember, soccer is a lot of little games inside the big game, so use simple, small-sided games. The ability of your players will dictate where you begin.

Build up the practice by adding attacking and defending players. When using small-sided games, you get better results when one or two goals are used. Remember to adjust the grid size when adding more players.

Illus. 79

Wrong

Right

There are four primary factors which influence the supporting distance:

• *The dribbling ability of the attacking player on the ball.* If the first marking defender player gets too tight and the supporting defender does not adjust his distance, the attacker may be able to go past both defending players.

• *The attacking player's physical speed.* Again, if the marking defender and the supporting defender get too tight, the attacking player may push the ball past them both and run into open space.

• *Position on the field.* The closer to the goal, the tighter every defender gets. But there may be times when the attacking player has been pushed into the corner of the field. When this happens, the defending team may apply pressure to the ball and all of the supporting players. By doing this, the defending team tries to deny time and space and force the attacking team to turn over the ball *(Illus. 80).*

• *Location of other defender.* A common fault is having a defender close an attacking player down, but his teammates fail to close down the supporting attacker. Remember that the supporting defender does not want to get caught too flat or square. The attacking player can then beat the defending player by the dribble and the 1-2.

• *Communication.* The supporting player must give verbal instruction to the pressuring player.

Illus. 80

Concentration

Illus. 81. Since the primary objective is to prevent goals, defenders must restrict the space from which their opponents can score. They can do this by retreating and concentrating the players in the defense third, or "danger area." Imagine two lines, 30 to 35 yards in length, joined by an arc and projected outward onto the field of play from each goal post at a 45° angle to the goal lines.

players, 20 yards is well within range. Everything's relative.

Funnelling or Recovery Runs

While a team is on attack, the players will usually be spread across the field. But once the ball is lost, the defending players begin to retreat to their own goal. The more they retreat the more they become centralized to

Illus. 81

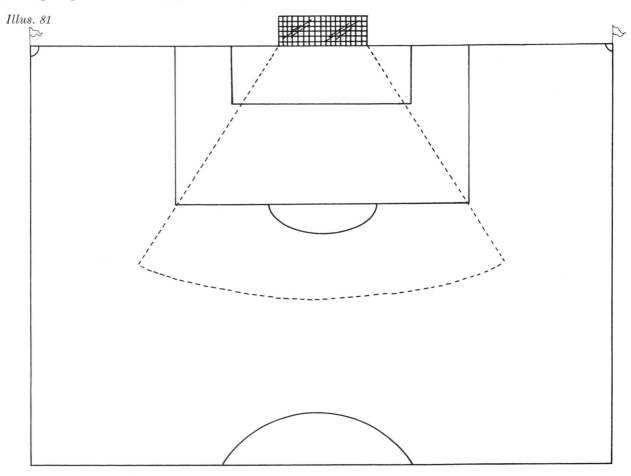

The threat that any shot poses from within this danger area depends largely on three factors: the distance from the goal that the shot is taken; by whom it is taken; and the angle from which it is taken. Obviously, young club players pose a very slight scoring threat from 25 yards out. But for world class

their own goal. This retreat is referred to as funnelling, or recovery runs.

Illus. 82. Funnelling or recovery runs are necessary so that the defending players will track back to defend the goal and the central space in front of the goal.

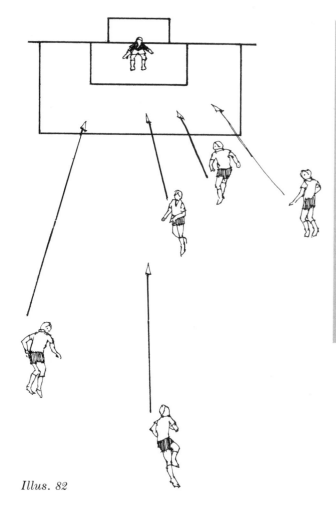

Illus. 82

Practice:

Start with a group tactical organization. A two-on-two in a 20-yard by 30-yard grid with two goals is good. Work with your players so that if they get beat by the dribble or by the pass they turn and recover at speed to their goal to reorganize. As your players get better at this tactic, add more players to the game.

The next step will be to move to a team tactical stage—a seven-on-seven, an eight-on-eight, or a nine-on-nine, with the same defensive requirement, but now involving more players so that when the attacking team loses possession of the ball, they must turn and recover to their goal at speed.

• *Mental concentration.* It takes great concentration to handle the switching from attacking to defending. If a defender hesitates, he will not have the time to recover.

• *Talking.* Verbal communication is very important to successful defending, especially when defenders are switching and recovering at speed.

• *Recover at speed.* When recovery is required, the defender must do so at speed.

• *Recover to the center of the goal.* Defending players must recover to the center of the goal.

Balance

Defending teams must cover the space which attacking teams may try to exploit. To assure the maintenance of proper marking of space at all times, a team must balance its defense and spread out across the field, protecting the most important areas.

Teams are unbalanced by their opponents in two ways: the use of mobility (running off the ball) to draw defenders out of position; or quickly changing the field of play and point of attack.

Practice:

Start with numbers-up possession games: four-on-two, six-on-four, or nine-on-six, in the proper grid size. In these games concentrate on the defensive shape of your team.

Small-sided games and numbers-up attack versus defense are helpful for demonstrating the necessity of defensive balance as well as how and when it breaks down. Use one-on-two, three-on-two, and six-on-four zone games.

• *Avoid getting caught square.* If balance is to be maintained, the defender cannot get caught square. Defenders must maintain depth.

• *Numbers up around the ball.* Defenders must try to get numbers up around the ball, but always try to maintain depth.

• *Closer to goal.* As attackers get closer to the goal, the tighter one must mark attacking players.

• *Avoid marking the least dangerous player.* By marking the least dangerous player too tightly, the defending team will throw the team balance out of whack (*Illus. 83*).

Illus. 83

V Midfield

Illus. 84. Many coaches call the midfield the engine room of their team. Even in the 1986 World Cup, many teams played with five midfielders. However, with all this emphasis on the importance of midfield play, not much is written about developing it.

Illus. 84

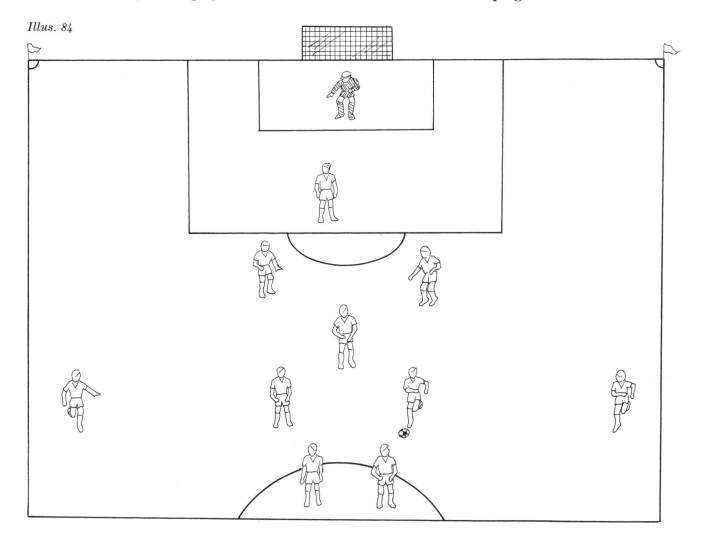

Transition

The first job of the midfielder is to provide an easy transition from the back players to the strikers. The hardest part of this job is mentally switching from defense to attack and quickly getting into position to provide outlets to back players and goalkeepers. Soccer as previously stated, is a game of time and space. If a team, especially at midfield, is in tune to the mental switching from defense to attack, it will find more time and space.

Illus. 85

Illus. 85. Midfield players must learn to make themselves available to back players and goalkeepers, or to do "showing," or support. This midfielder is providing an option for the man on the ball.

Midfielders are also required to provide support to all front players. For example, if the front players receive service from one of the back players, the midfielder must get into a supporting role.

A good practice to help develop the mental and physical transition is a zone game—for fullbacks and a goalkeeper against two strikers. The fullbacks and goalkeepers try to work the ball into the three or four midfielders who are playing against two defending midfielders. Add or subtract players depending on their success and as the practice develops. This makes the practice as much like a game condition as possible.

Coaching Points

• *Showing*. Train the midfielders to anticipate the play and to show early—to get into an early supporting position for their teammates. By doing this they will increase their time and space on the ball. Do not hide behind defenders.

• *The mental transition from attack to defense*. Probably the most difficult skill to learn is the continuous switching from attack to defense and back again. This skill must be practised in the game situation, five on-five, etc.

• *Body position*. Train the midfield players to receive the ball facing the field of play as much as possible. Much of the time the body position will be 90° when the ball is received. Many times young midfielders will receive the ball with their back to the opposition goal, and this makes them blind to opponents.

Tempo of Play

The midfield is responsible for setting the team's tempo of play and it takes great experience to know when and how to change this. The game can become so fast that players start to react to the ball and not to the whole situation. There is no time to think when players are running wild and the ball is flying around. This turns the game into high tempo kickball. The midfield must be able to bring the ball under control and slow the game down when necessary.

Illus. 86. One reason that the game speeds up so much and midfielders are forced to play the ball so early is the lack of space at midfield. The midfielder must have the ability to bring the ball under control and spread the game out by playing a pass back or wide. This will spread the game out and allow for needed space to be used. The pass which plays back on wide is what I call a *possession pass.*

The midfielder must also learn when it is advantageous to speed the game up. The problem, however, is learning *how* to speed the game up by making the right decision and not just by kicking the ball recklessly.

A classic example of a team that plays a slow tempo, changing at the right moment to a high tempo is Brazil. The Brazilians will maintain possession of the ball, probe the opponents' defense, even lulling them to

sleep, and then explode in an attacking, penetrating move, such as a long ball or quick 1–2 around the box.

Practice:

Slow build-up, to slow the tempo. The purpose of this training is to get into midfield quickly, and, once there, to get the midfielder's help in slowing the tempo down. The organization is 3 grids divided equally into 3 zones, with 3 teams of 4. Team One brings the ball into the zone, that Team Two is defending. Team One tries to work the ball into the free zone. Once there, they organize and enter the third zone, which is defended by Team Three. Team One enters the third zone with the intent of scoring a goal. If Team Two wins possession of the ball before Team One can enter the free zone, then Team Two tries to score with Team One defending. If Team One wins back possession of the ball, they try to get into the free zone. Once they have entered the third zone, Team Three will defend and stop Team One from scoring. If Team Two wins possession of the ball or is scored on, they must try to get the ball into the free zone (*Illus. 87*).

Coaching Points

• *Get into midfield early.* The ball must be played into the midfield early and quickly. The supporting midfield player must get to midfield quickly, so that the man on the ball has options and also numbers up to maintain possession.

• *Proper supporting distance.* Here again support is needed, but not so much that the man on the ball is smothered by killing his time and space, or by bringing in additional defenders.

• *Slow the tempo down.* Once the player gets into midfield, slow the tempo down in order to keep possession of the ball and allow additional players to get forward.

Illus. 87

Quick Tempo

When the ball is won, the attacking team wants to break out of midfield as quickly as possible, and at the same time get players ahead of the ball to support the players in midfield. Again, reading the situation on the field is the key. If they see that they have the opportunity to get numbers up, they must break out quickly and get supporting players ahead of the ball.

Practice:

Illus. 88. Have two teams with the field divided in two. Before a team can score a goal, the entire attacking team must be in the attacking half of the field.

Illus. 88

58

• *Playing the balls early forward.* When a player wins possession, he should play the ball quickly forward, preferably into the striker; by doing so, he will take more defending players out of the game.

• *Proper supporting distance.* Do not smother the man on the ball by killing his time and space, but do provide options for him.

• *Running into space.* When balls are played early and quickly, the art of third person running can be very effective in penetrating. It also provides more options of support.

Balance

Midfield balance at the youth level is difficult to teach for many reasons: concepts of time, space, and support are hard to get across; everyone wants to score and no one wants to defend, and the switching from offense to defense is tricky.

Illus. 89. Balance problems in the midfield occur in two ways. One is when the midfield becomes too flat, or lacks depth, the midfield players push too far into the attack, crowding the front players. The other is when the ball is cleared from the defense, those midfielders must turn and chase down the opposing players and the ball.

Illus. 89

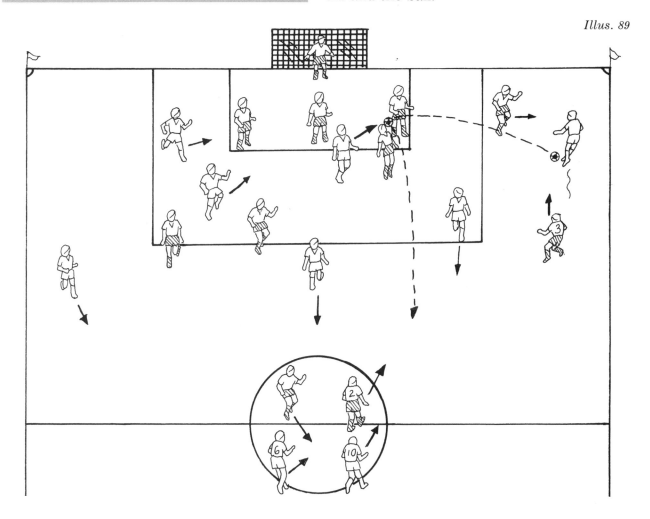

This can also happen when the ball is brought down the wing and crossed. Everyone pushes so tightly towards the goal that no one is left around the top of the box for rebounds and poor clearances.

Lack of width is also a problem. This usually happens when players crowd around the ball. In this case, patience on the player's part is very important. If he goes inside looking for the ball, he will kill the time and space for himself and his teammates.

Coaching Points

• *Time and space.* Train the midfield to maximize the time and space available to them and avoid getting into the habit of killing the space too early.
• *Support.* Train the midfield to know when to support and to judge the proper supporting distance.
• *Avoid a flat midfield.* Make sure midfielders understand the need for depth in the midfield.

Possession

Goal scoring can be accomplished only with possession of the ball; thus, the most important principle in soccer is to maintain possession of the ball as much as possible.

Illus. 90. When coaches talk about retaining possession, they sometimes overlook how. First, the supporting players must read the play, or situation, and react to it. They must see the ball being played and get into an early supporting position before the ball is received by their teammates, because the player receiving the ball must concentrate on his first touch. Many times the first touch (or lack of first touch) causes players to lose possession of the ball, lose scoring opportunities, and even risk injury when trying to regain possession. The first touch should only keep the ball moving and out of tight areas. When a player gets the ball from a teammate in a tight area, he must come completely out of the area rather than sending the ball back into it. This is a common fault of young players.

Illus. 90

Another key element in retaining possession is playing simply and quickly in the direction you are facing. There are many ways to maintain possession of the ball: proper support, switching of play, wall passes, take overs, and dribbling.

Proper Support

Illus. 91. One of the main jobs of the midfielder is to support the man on the ball. However, a team can over-support by having too many players around the man on the ball. When teammates do this, they also bring defending players with them. This, in turn, decreases time and space for the attacking team.

Another way to over-support is by being too close or too far away from the man on the ball. If the supporting player is too close, he will bring an extra defender into the play, and thus not provide himself with time and space, because when the ball is played to the supporting player, the defending player can easily slide from the passer to the supporting player. If the supporting players are too far way, the man with the ball won't find the supporting player. The player will then lose possession by trying to hold on to the ball or his pass will be interrupted.

Practice:

Three-on-one; four-on-two: five-on-five; six-on four; all keep away games.

Illus. 91

• *Be ready*. Get into good early supporting position before the ball arrives.

• *Over-supporting*. Do not over-support the player with the ball by bringing too many players to the ball. By doing this the attack will lose its shape.

• *Find the right supporting distance*. If the supporting player gets too close, he will bring defending players to the man on the ball. This will close down the time and space. If the supporting player is too far away, the man on the ball will have difficulty in finding supporting help.

• *Proper support angles*: Many times the supporting players will not provide the player on the ball enough of a supporting angle. Coach players to provide the proper angle and not to hide behind defenders or get lazy.

Switching of Play

One of the big problems of youth midfield players is that they tend to play balls into tight areas or back into the area they just came from. For example, a midfielder will go into a supporting position and receive a pass which should be turned and switched, but instead will try to force it back into the same area it came from. The player must learn to look around while the ball is on its way. This way, he will know what to do with it when he receives it.

Practice:

Short-short-long. In this practice, have two teams playing keep away in the proper grid size for the number of players used. Every third pass must be a long pass. Switching of play or point of attack.

• *Anticipating what to do with the ball*. Instill players with the habit of deciding what to do with the ball before they receive it.

• *Looking around*. Teach the players to take a quick look around as the ball comes to them.

• *Body position*. Players should not play with their backs to the field when they receive a pass. They should try to be in a position to see the field.

Going Forward

Coaches all agree that one of the jobs of the midfielder is to assist in goal scoring. Youth players often break down in this area.

Illus. 92

Illus. 92. How often does a great attacking move break down because the final pass from the midfielder is not accurate? The pass is either too hard, too soft, too late, too early or it may have been flighted when it should have been on the ground. Should the pass be into space or to feet? These are some of the decisions which the midfielder must make in a tenth of a second and execute. In most cases, the forward is running away from the midfielder, which poses another problem for the midfielder—hitting a moving target!

Practice:

Six attackers on five defenders going to goal. Use a game condition trying to isolate the midfielders and the decisions they will have to make. As the midfielders gain competence, add more attacking and defending midfielders to the practice.

Illus. 94

Coaching Points

- *Eye contact.* Making eye contact is very important. Each player must know where the others are going.
- *Time of release.* The midfielder must learn to release the pass at the right moment.
- *Type of pass.* Train midfielders to know what type of pass to make and what part of the foot they may use.
- *Shot on goal.* When one sees the goal, one must be prepared to shoot.

Illus. 94–95. This is a two-part move, starting with the player with the ball. The defender must keep the player with the ball from dribbling past him. Thus, the player on the ball must be directed to release his pass to the wall at the right time. If he releases too early, the defender can turn and recover and stop the second pass *(Illus. 94)*. If he releases too late, the ball can be intercepted *(Illus. 95)*.

Wall Pass

Illus. 93. One of the most elementary moves in the game of soccer is the wall pass, or the give and go, or 1–2. Many young players miss this tactic and it shows up later.

Illus. 95

Illus. 93

Illus. 96

Illus. 96. The next piece of the puzzle is to get the player on the wall coordinated with the player on the ball. If the wall receives the ball too far away, the defending player can turn and recover. The wall players must be prepared to move to reduce the distance the ball must travel on its two passing movements.

Sometimes the wall player will hide behind the defender and fail to provide the proper passing angle. If the wall player stands even with the defender, the offsider rule may come into effect. So the wall player must play a little in front of the defender to provide a proper angle.

Practice:

Use the players as walls so that the players inside can play off them to create 1–2's. After the fast practice, add more players and goals *(Illus. 97)*.

Coaching Points

• Convince the defender that the attacker is prepared to dribble past him by running at him at speed.
• Make eye contact.
• Release the ball at the right time.
• Accelerate past the defender.
• Wall manages proper distance and angle for the pass.

Illus. 97

Take Over

The take over occurs when a player takes control of the ball from a teammate. The purpose of the take over is to free a player from a defender or to penetrate towards the goal.

Illus. 98. To execute the take over, the attacking player with the ball must convince the defending player who is marking him that he is trying to run past him going to goal. This commits the defender to the attacking player who is trying to penetrate.

Illus. 99. The attacking player must find a team-mate who, in turn, must see what is developing and react to the situation. When these two players come together there must be some communication between them—usually the word "leave" or "take."

Illus. 100. A big problem is that after the communication has been made, the attacking player with the ball often tries to take another touch and pass the ball to the player who is taking over. This ruins the rhythm and timing, and the ball is usually lost to the other team. Once the communication has occurred, the attacking player with the ball should leave it alone. Remember that the attacking player should always carry the ball from the outside foot, using his body as a shield from the defender. When the take over has been completed, both players should accelerate, but not in a straight line. Many players execute a take over, but they never really try to penetrate.

Illus. 100

Illus. 101

Illus. 101. As the take over is being executed, the first touch should be either in a positive move, or a penetrating move towards the goal into the space behind the defender.

66

Illus. 102

Illus. 102. Many times the take over is made with the attacking player taking the ball over and going to goal, but the player who has left the ball still continues to run square and does not get the ball back.

Illus. 103

Illus. 103. Now the player who has taken the ball over will have many options. He can take an early shot at goal; pass the ball back to the teammate running there; or continue to penetrate by the dribble. After a player has perfected the take over, he can add a fake take over. Everything is the same as the take over except that the attacking player keeps the ball instead of giving it up. The player in position reads the defender and keeps the ball.

Practice:

Two-on-two plus one.

Coaching Points

- Communication.
- Avoid extra or confusing touches by team in possession.
- Change of pace at take over.
- Change of direction by receiving player.

- First player keeps the ball if defender reads it.
- Supporting player times run at correct movement.
- Fake take over.

VI   Principles of Play

Before a coach can teach and develop tactics, he must understand the principles of the game of soccer—the "principles of play."

Width

Since the primary objective of defending players is to deny space to their opponent's attack, attacking players must counteract this through the principle of width.

Every attacking player is looking for space, because space means time. Width achieves more space. This involves not only wingers, but also outside midfielders and outside backs. When a team is attacking, the players spread out to create as much space as possible. This causes the defending team to spread out to cover the attackers. When the defending team spreads out, space is created on the inside, which gives central players more time and less pressure.

Practice:

The free zone game. The team plays in half the field and a free zone area is marked out on both touch lines.

Illus. 104. The team with possession of the ball can either dribble or pass into the free area. Once there, the defending team cannot enter. Therefore, the team with possession of the ball can go anywhere in the free area without pressure of opponents. Change the practice any way that suits the need. For example, have the attacking team use the free zone only in their attacking half of the field without pressure of opponents. Another restriction would be that all goals scored must come from service from the free zone.

Remember when using these practices that they are done as realistically as possible. Sometimes when using this practice, players have a tendency to get out in the free zone and become lazy and unrealistic, possibly walking, taking too many touches on the ball or hiding.

The coach can cure this by imposing a touch limitation on how many touches can be taken while in the free zone—example 3, 4, or 5 if there is a violation the ball is turned over to the other team. He can also limit the number of players in the free zone at one time. This should keep too many players from going into the free zone to hide. Remember, too, as the coach you should demand that all play in the free zone is done realistically and at speed. Another good method for developing width is a game called possession. Two teams (seven-on-seven or eight-on-eight) are in a large grid usually 60 yards by 40 yards or half field. The

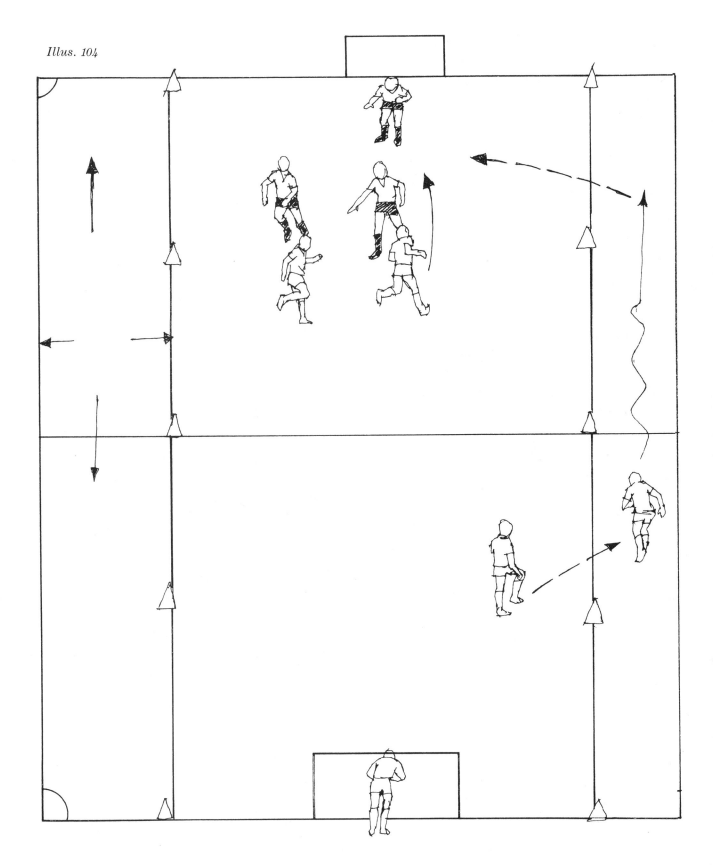

object of this game is for the two teams to keep the ball from each other and maintain possession of it—a large keep away game. Because there are no goals, there will be no predetermined direction of the game, so the direction of the game is ever changing. This will give the players and the coach many opportunities to apply the width element to the practice.

Depth

While there is width in attack, there is none in defense, since the object is to limit time and space. However, while there is some depth in attack by pushing players forward, there is *true* depth in defense, when players are backing up or supporting other players around the ball. Thus, if the attacking team does not have depth in their attack, it becomes flat as well as having less time and space.

Illus. 105

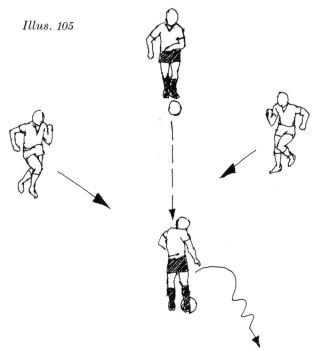

Illus. 105. If there is no depth in attack, there can be no penetrating passes. Thus, many defending players will not be taken out of the game by having the ball played past them.

Adding depth will stretch the defending team from front to back, and from left to right. This will create much more time and space for the team and will demand more of the defending team.

Practice:

The best way I have found to develop depth in attack is the constant reminder in small-sided games and practice games. A coach must be prepared to stop the practice and go in to show reasons *why* the team needs depth in its attack.

Penetration

Penetration usually refers to balls or passes (for example, a through pass for an attacking player to turn on). If teams always play around the perimeter of the defense, they will never put defending players out of the game by attempting the penetrating pass (and will never score, either). A penetrating pass does not have to be played towards the opponent's goal to be considered a penetrating pass. It does take opponents out of the game at the moment in which it is made. A good example of this would be a player using a long ball to switch the play.

Illus. 106. How many times does a player receive a pass from a teammate when he is in a gap, but, instead of turning and moving into space, he goes back and keeps those two players in the game. Thus, the defending players do not have to turn and chase. This happens a lot in the midfield area.

When coaches talk about penetration, they seldom mean the penetration of *players*. Rather, they talk about the penetration of balls in play. For example, when most teams are on the attack, they usually have three players ahead of the ball and eight behind or even with the ball in the attacking third of the field.

Coaches need to encourage penetration of forward players. The Italians, for example, are very good at this. They play their soccer very straight ahead. When they win possession of the ball, teammates will sprint forward into a penetrating and supporting position all the way down the field. When attacking, it is best to get numerical advantage in the attack as quickly as possible, so that the defending team won't have time to organize itself.

Illus. 107. Another more exciting, type of penetration is *dribbling*. A good dribbler can break down the best-organized defenses in the world, not to mention their morale and spirit.

Illus. 107

Illus. 108

Illus. 108. Another form of penetration is what some coaches call "running with the ball." This differs from dribbling in that running with the ball is simply running into open space, while dribbling involves actually taking on opposing players.

Running with the ball involves getting forward as soon as possible. How quickly a player can get forward will determine how many players a coach can take out of the game for that particular move.

Practice:

Play a small-sided game (five-on-five, six-on-six, seven-on-seven) going to goal. When the player with the ball makes a pass to a teammate who is square or forward of him, the passer must sprint past the receiver into a penetrating position ahead of the ball. This practice will also sharpen third person running. Remember this is a physically demanding practice, so as the coach be prepared to vocally encourage your players.

Mobility

The principle of mobility can be broken down into two areas, team mobility and individual mobility.

Illus. 109. Individual mobility does not refer to pure speed, which is the ability to cover a distance related to time, but the ability to cover the *right* distance at the right *tactical* time as with a player who is always moving or just standing around until the ball comes his way. Another example involves "unselfish running"—when a player, knowing he will not receive the ball, makes a run in order to open space for a teammate to use.

Illus. 109

Illus. 110. Here, the right wing has made a diagonal run towards the center of the field. Now the fullback must decide to go with the runner or stay where he is. If he goes with the runner, then a large space is now open to be exploited, and in this case the right midfielder has chosen to make a run forward into open space. Note that the attacking midfielder made his run *behind* the defending midfielder, waiting until the defending midfielder completely turned his back. Also, take note that the right wing may run in *front* of the defending fullback, so that the defending fullback is aware of the winger's run. The rule is this: If a player is trying to take someone out of a space, he runs in front so that the opponent can see him. If he is trying to run away or lose the defender, he runs behind the opponent if possible.

Illus. 110

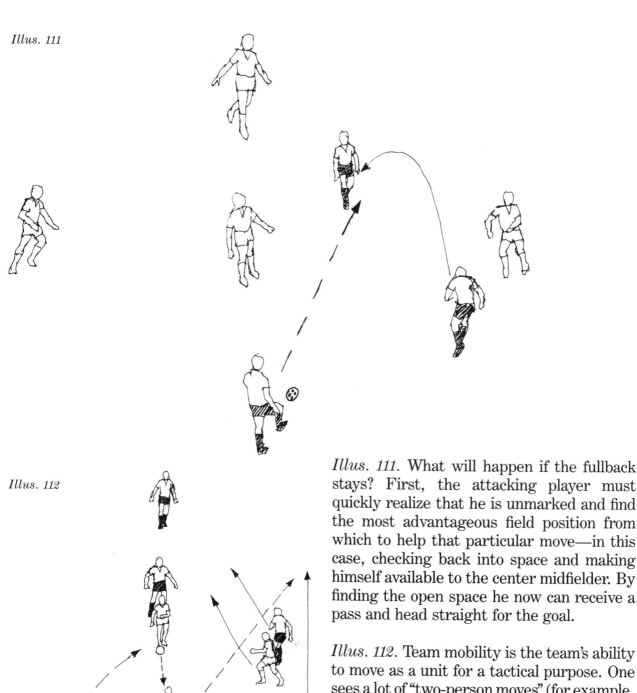

Illus. 111. What will happen if the fullback stays? First, the attacking player must quickly realize that he is unmarked and find the most advantageous field position from which to help that particular move—in this case, checking back into space and making himself available to the center midfielder. By finding the open space he now can receive a pass and head straight for the goal.

Illus. 112. Team mobility is the team's ability to move as a unit for a tactical purpose. One sees a lot of "two-person moves" (for example, a simple 1–2 with a teammate), but not a lot of "third-person running" in club soccer. For example, a center striker receives the ball from the fullback, which he lays back to a supporting midfielder. In turn, the supporting midfielder plays a through pass to the right side midfielder, who is making a run forward. Another example is when large gaps start to appear in the midfield area, caused by midfielders attacking and fullbacks not filling in to keep the team compact and time and space limited.

In order for mobility to be a positive factor, players must have a complete understanding of all the principles of play. Once this has been accomplished, the coach must mould these players into a functioning unit by asking them questions which stimulate their thinking.

Support

A team must have possession of the ball before it can score goals. But possession is not enough. A team's ability to *maintain* possession of the ball is also critical.

Illus. 113. The most important factor in maintaining possession of the ball is support of the player who has the ball—providing the player on the ball with options. If a player loses possession of the ball it was probably because he didn't have any support from his teammates. Does this mean that any time one of the players has possession of the ball, the rest of the team should swamp him? On the contrary—two or three players at a favorable supporting distance is plenty. If too many supporting players are brought around the ball, defending players are brought to the ball as well, so don't oversupport the player with possession of the ball.

Illus. 113

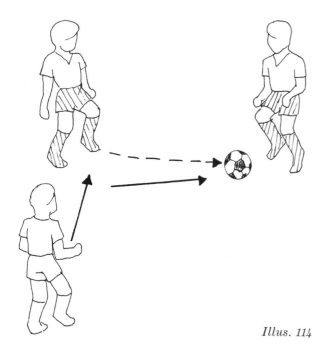

Illus. 114.

Illus. 114. When supporting the player with the ball, don't get too close. If a support player receives a pass, the defender who is marking the player with possession can close down on the support player.

It should be clear by now that the player with the ball needs close support, but what about long support? The player with the ball needs this option if he desires to use it. The switching of play, or attack, can be very effective in creating gaps within defenses. Therefore, the player on the ball needs long support as well as short support.

Practice:

Use small-sided games such as three-on-one, three-on-two, four-on-two, all in the proper sized grid. By working in this fashion, the coach can concentrate on early support to be already in place before the ball arrives.

An effective practice for developing support for a team is a simple keep away game with restrictions. With two teams in half a field, make the team in possession play a pattern of two short passes, always followed by one long pass. This restriction forces them to play the long supporting pass, which will force players into correct position for long support.

Creativity and Improvisation

Illus. 115. A true mark of a great team is the ability to do the unexpected during a match. However, in order for players to perform the unexpected, they must be technically sound. Improvisation is usually a modification of a skill.

Illus. 115

Practice:

Teaching improvisation is difficult. I recommend playing games around the goal in tight areas, with high pressure of opponents and limited time and space. By imposing such an environment, a coach forces his players to think and react more quickly. Encourage creativity in the players. The player must not be hesitant to try new things for fear that the coach is going to yell at him. Challenge players to be creative and adventurous.

Overlapping

Overlapping is a soccer tactic which brings players from a supporting position behind the ball to a supporting position ahead of the ball. This move is mostly executed by defenders and midfielders coming forward.

Illus. 116

Illus. 116. The first concern of the overlapping player is when to or when not to overlap. It is safe to say that most overlapping runs are made in numbers-up situations around the ball for the attacking team, usually two-on-one.

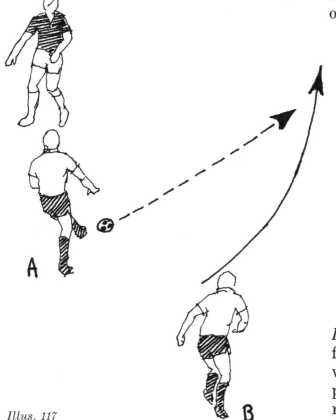

Illus. 117

Illus. 117. Consider the availability of space for the overlapping player to run into. It would be difficult to overlap if the overlapping player is marked tightly and has no space to run into.

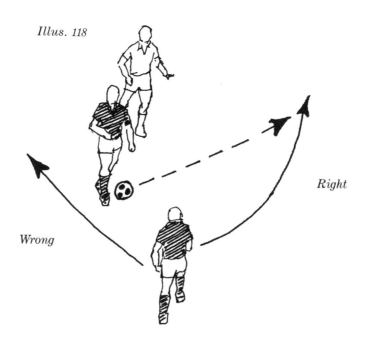

Illus. 118

Wrong

Right

Illus. 118. A common fault with young players is to run on the inside of the player in possession of the ball, when he should be running on the outside of that player. Doing this creates time and space for himself.

Illus. 119. As soon as the overlapping player decides to overlap he must communicate this to his teammate who is in possession of the ball. This is important because a lot of times the player in possession of the ball has his back to the overlapping player.

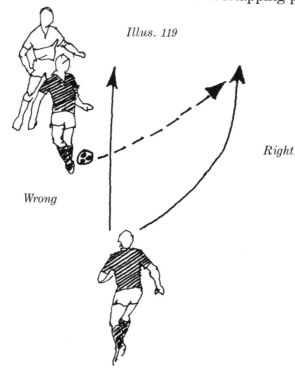

Illus. 119

Wrong

Right

The timing of the overlapping run is very important. If the runner goes too early he may run into an offside position. If he waits too long he may find that the defender has closed to tackle his teammate who is in possession of the ball.

The next phase of the overlapping move is the width of the overlapping runner around the player in possession of the ball. If the overlapping player runs in a straight line by his teammate then the probability of interception is great. The overlapping player should run wide of the player in possession, thus creating time and space between him and the nearest defender. Also, by running wide it provides space for the pass to be played into.

Illus. 120

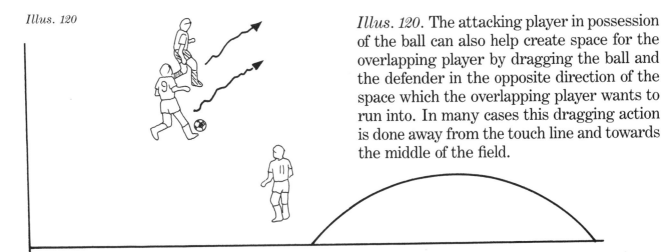

Illus. 120. The attacking player in possession of the ball can also help create space for the overlapping player by dragging the ball and the defender in the opposite direction of the space which the overlapping player wants to run into. In many cases this dragging action is done away from the touch line and towards the middle of the field.

Illus. 121

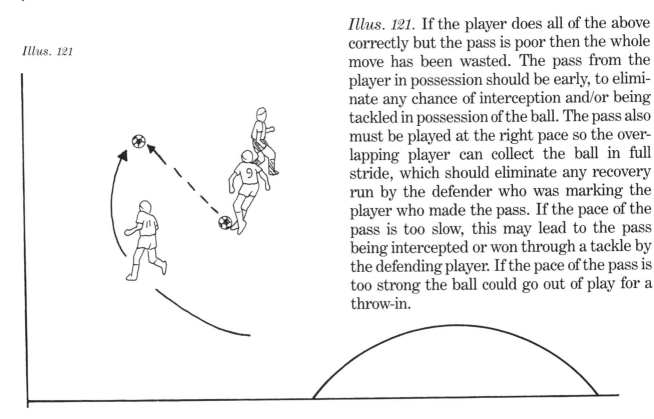

Illus. 121. If the player does all of the above correctly but the pass is poor then the whole move has been wasted. The pass from the player in possession should be early, to eliminate any chance of interception and/or being tackled in possession of the ball. The pass also must be played at the right pace so the overlapping player can collect the ball in full stride, which should eliminate any recovery run by the defender who was marking the player who made the pass. If the pace of the pass is too slow, this may lead to the pass being intercepted or won through a tackle by the defending player. If the pace of the pass is too strong the ball could go out of play for a throw-in.

Practice:

A simple pattern play.

Illus. 122. Have three lines of players at midfield facing goal, with a goalkeeper as the only opposition. Three players line up so that one player is out wide and the two other players are at the far and near posts. The player at the near post position has the ball to start. He plays the ball out to the wide player for him to control and drag the ball to the inside of the field. This player then follows his pass and makes the overlapping run, receiving the ball back from the wide player to get the cross in. The player that was out wide makes the near post run and the player lined up on the far post makes a late looping run to the far post.

Illus. 122

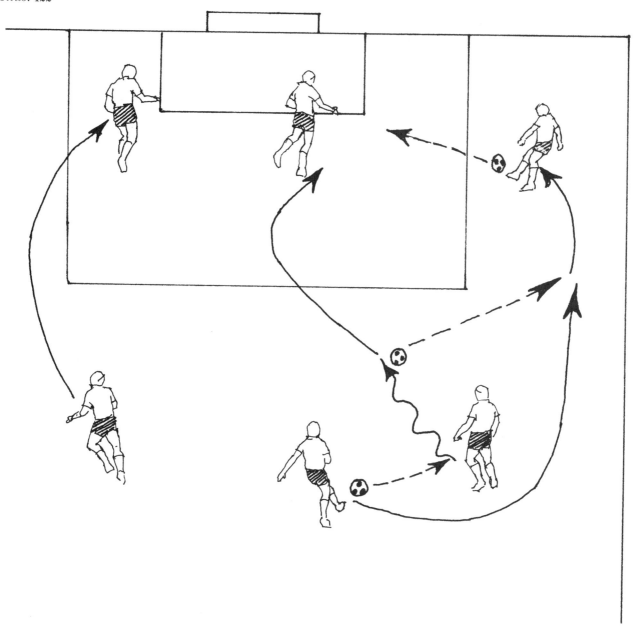

• To pick the right tactical time to overlap, concerning the right number of players and the availability of space to run into.
• Communication, telling the player in possession of the ball that you are overlapping.
• To overlap on the outside of the player in possession of the ball.
• The proper timing of the overlapping run.
• Proper width between the overlapping player and the player in possession of the ball.
• The player in possession of the ball to help create space by dragging the ball and the defender away from the space that the overlapping player wants to run into.
• The proper timing and weight of the pass.

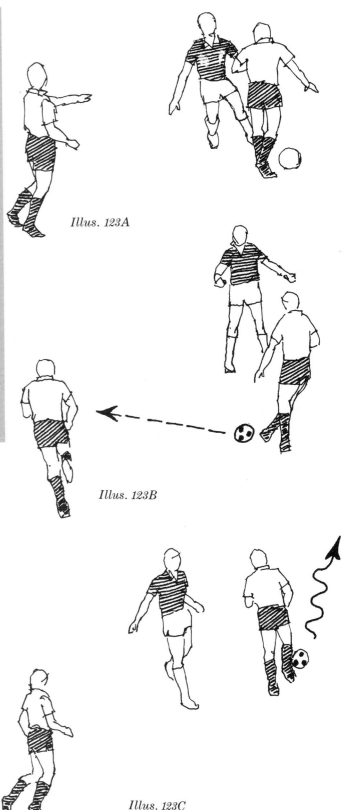

Illus. 123A

Illus. 123B

Illus. 123C

Defending Against Two-on-One

Two-on-one situations arise often, but working on defending this situation is often neglected.

Illus. 123. In the two-on-one, there are only three ways that the attacking player can beat the defender. He can dribble by the defender, pass the ball to a supporting player, or, if he's close enough to the defending player he can push the ball wide of him to create space for a shot on goal.

• Don't have players rush in and sell themselves. By doing this a goal should be scored.

• Have the defender try and slow down the two attacking players by delaying. This can be done by simple retreating towards the defended goal. However, the defender cannot retreat into his own goal; eventually he will have to make a stand. Delaying will also reduce the space behind the defender for the attacking two to exploit. Finally, delaying will allow for defending teammates to make recovery runs to help the lone defender.

• The defender should position himself so that he is inviting the attacking player to pass the ball to his supporting teammate. By making the two attacking players pass the ball the attack will slow down. This will let the defending players track back and help, as well as increase the likelihood of the two attacking players making a mistake (a bad pass, or poor control) which could lead to the ball being won by the defender.

• Have the defending player position himself to cut off the pass to the supporting attacking player and invite the attacking player in possession to dribble by him. Some coaches consider this a poor defensive tactic, but by defending in this fashion the defender is in the driver's seat to dictate to the attacking player. Both players know there is only one way to beat the defender—through the dribble. When the attacking player tries to do this, the defender can win the ball through the tackle. If not, the defender should try to push the attacking player as wide as possible to decrease his shooting angle at goal, making it easier for the goalkeeper to save.

VII Shooting

How many times has a team stood in disbelief after a teammate does not shoot on goal when he has a clear opportunity? Doesn't he know that he will never score if he never shoots? What is the use of a great build-up if no one is prepared to take responsibility for shooting? This is where coaches must demand that players take responsibility for shooting, and not worry about missing. It is up to the coach to create the right psychological environment for players to shoot and not be afraid of missing.

To be a successful goal scorer one must take responsibility for shooting; be selfish in front of the goal; take the first opportunity to shoot the ball; be brave and be prepared to run at defenders and get into the penalty box at every chance; and convert any half chances (bouncing balls) which arise in the goals. All goal scoring opportunities seem to arise from either a defensive mistake or from the attacking team's ability to create scoring opportunities through their play.

Obviously, scoring goals is the most important element in soccer. This, then, makes shooting on goal the second most important element. Attacking players score goals from five types of service: the ball moving towards the shooter; the ball moving away from the shooter; the ball moving across the shooter; the half chances (bouncing balls, half volleys, etc.); the service which is taken out of the air (full volley).

The ball moving towards the shooter is always in danger of being shot over the bar. Because of its backward rotation, the ball must be struck through or slightly above the middle. When striking the ball remember that it does not have to be struck hard when moving toward the shooter. The force of the moving ball and the leg swing will provide plenty of power. Coach players to watch the ball, keep their heads down and their upper bodies over the ball. These will all help keep the shot down.

Illus. 124–128 (pages 84–85). When practising this technique remember to serve bouncing balls as well. When striking a bouncing ball concentrate on striking it on the way down.

Illus. 124

Practice:

Have the shooter pass the ball to a target player about 10 yards in front of him, who in turn plays the ball back to the shooter, who then shoots on goal.

Illus. 125

Illus. 128

Coaching Points

- Keep eye on the ball.
- Hit through the middle or upper half of the ball.
- Do not over strike the ball.
- On bouncing balls, hit the ball on the way down.
- Keep head down and upper body over the ball.
- Make sure the plant foot is near and a little behind the ball.
- Try to land on the shooting foot.
- Hit the target.

The ball moving away from the shooter is much easier to keep low because of its forward rotation.

Illus. 129–134. These types of balls occur around the penalty box where attacking players will lay balls off to players running through, usually because the ball has been passed on for players to run onto. Remember to practise striking bouncing balls as well.

Illus. 129

Illus. 130

Illus. 131

Illus. 133

Illus. 132

Illus. 134

Practice:

Have a serving player stand behind the shooting player. The server passes the ball on the ground past the shooting player for him to run onto and to shoot on goal. Have the serving player serve bouncing balls for the shooter to shoot on goal.

Illus. 135

Illus. 136

Coaching Points

- Keep eye on the ball.
- Hit through the middle or upper half of the ball.
- Do not over strike the ball.
- On bouncing balls, hit the ball on the way down.
- Keep head down and upper body over the ball.
- Make sure the plant foot is near and a little behind the ball.
- Try to land on the shooting foot.
- Hit the target.

The ball moving across the face of the shooter is by far the hardest to strike.

Illus. 135–137. The sweeping leg action and the timing needed to strike a ball which runs in front the shooter is a difficult technique to master. The shooting foot is nearest to the ball, with the plant foot placed in towards the target when contact is made. This is because one of the common mistakes is to open up the plant foot too much and drag the shot wide to the far post.

Practice:

Have a server pass balls across the face of the shooter. Remember to serve bouncing balls.

Illus. 137

Half chances bounce into (and out of) the penalty box. For every goal scored, the ball has to travel through the penalty box. Thus, it is from inside the penalty box that most goals come.

Illus. 138. A player has to be brave in the penalty box and convert these half chances into goals. It may require sticking one's head where there are only cleats. It is usually these half chances that win games, but coaches spend a very low percentage of training time devoted to this type of shooting. The coach must make practices as realistic as possible, in other words, work on improvisation. Coaches shouldn't stifle their players' imagination, but instead encourage them to come up with new ways in which to solve the problem of scoring goals. The more skillful the player, the greater range of improvisation he can achieve.

Illus. 138

Coaching Points

- Keep eye on the ball.
- Hit through the middle or upper half of the ball.
- Do not over strike the ball.
- On bouncing balls, hit the ball on the way down.
- Keep head down and upper body over the ball.
- Plant foot point towards the target.
- Hit the target.

Practice:

This practice is called "Kill the Goalkeeper." Start with small numbers (three-on-three) inside the penalty box, with the coach serving balls into the box. Vary the serve and have the player running inside the box, not standing (if players stand, do not serve the ball). During the practice add players until the entire team is involved. I have used this practice with 22 players, eleven-on-eleven. With so many players in the box, it will emphasize the speed of thinking, time and space *(Illus. 139)*.

Illus. 139

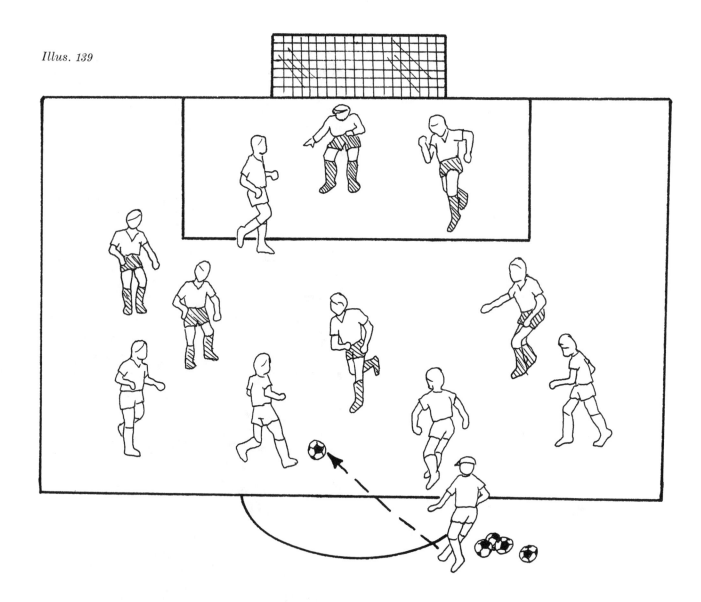

Scoring a goal from a full volley can be very exciting, though most of these chances go astray. The most important part of the execution of this skill is the preparation before the strike.

Illus. 140–143. The attacking player should almost turn his back to the goal that he is attacking; then step with the foot nearest to the ball, and plant this foot towards the target, dipping the shoulder nearest the ball. This will get his kicking leg up to be able to strike over and through the ball, thus keeping the shot down. It is important that the attacking player watch the ball until it makes contact and leaves his foot.

Illus. 140

Illus. 142

Illus. 141

Illus. 143

Practice:

Have a server hand serve balls for the shooter to strike out of the air. The server should stand 5 to 7 yards away from the shooter, moving farther back from the shooter as he improves. Remember to serve balls from both sides. Again after proficiency is met then have your player handle ball from a greater distance and from a foot serve *(Illus. 144–145)*.

Illus. 144

Illus. 145

Illus. 146

Illus. 147

Illus. 146. Players should always make the goalkeeper save the shot. The shot might rebound off the goalkeeper, post or crossbar. If this happens, the opportunity for the second-chance goal is always there. Better to miss wide than high. A wide shot always has a chance for deflection that could go in the goal, find a runner to the back post, or just simply keep the ball alive. A high shot only goes for a goalkick.

Illus. 147. Players have to be brave and be prepared to get into the penalty box at every opportunity, knowing that they are going to be held, pushed and kicked, but once they are in the penalty box with the possession of the ball, the defending team must handle them with kid gloves. If not, there will be a foul, a penalty kick will be awarded and surely a goal will be scored.

- Get body into a ready position early.
- Identify the path of the ball in flight.
- Turn the plant foot towards the goal.
- Watch the ball all the way in and off one foot.
- Dip the nearest shoulder.
- Hit through the top half or middle of the ball.

Defending Goal Shots

Four defensive mistakes usually produce goals: failing to apply pressure to the man on the ball; failing to track down attacking players who go on penetrating runs; failing to provide defensive support and depth; and failing to maintain possession of the ball, especially in one's defensive third of the field.

Illus. 148. Lack of pressure on the man with the ball is the primary cause of goals scored. This enables the attacking players to analyze the situation and punish the other team by shooting on goal, or providing a good pass that will lead to a shot on goal. If pressure is applied to the man on the ball, his time and space will be limited. This will put pressure on the skill level and tactical decision making. It will also stop him from making any penetrating pass because the passing lanes will be cut down.

If an attacking player shoots on the first opportunity, he may miss the goal, but, then again, he may not. The first shooting opportunity is usually the best one. Trying to improve chances might force the team into a worse position in relationship to the goal, or worse, cause them to lose possession of the ball.

Illus. 148

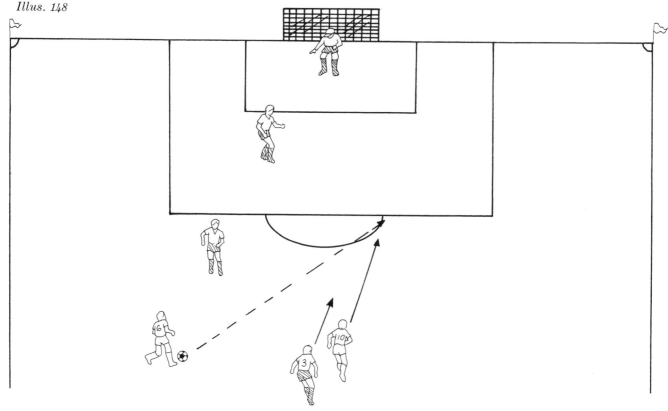

Illus. 149. Although front players are usually marked tight, too often defenders let attacking players making penetrating runs from behind the ball go unmarked. Most of these runs come from the fullback and midfield area because the defending players are ball-watching, or choosing not to track the player down.

Illus. 149

Illus. 150. The defending players must provide support and depth in defense. This enables the defense to apply pressure and restrict time and space to the man on the ball. By providing depth, the defense limits the space which can be exploited behind them. With this support the pressuring defenders can go on with the job of pressuring the man on the ball.

Illus. 150

Failure to hold onto the ball after winning possession is a fault at any level. Losing the ball in the defensive third of the field can be devastating. For example, the first goal given away by Denmark against Spain in the 1986 World Cup tied the game 1–1, with Denmark never recovering and losing 5–1. The ball can be lost through a bad tactical decision, or a technical breakdown. Coaches should preach "safety first" at all times in the defending third. This includes playing the ball back to the goalkeeper if necessary to get out of trouble.

More Shooting Practices

Illus. 151. Simply shooting at goal with the coach laying balls off to the shooter. Perform

this practice from various angles. Also, remember to vary the layoff.

Illus. 151

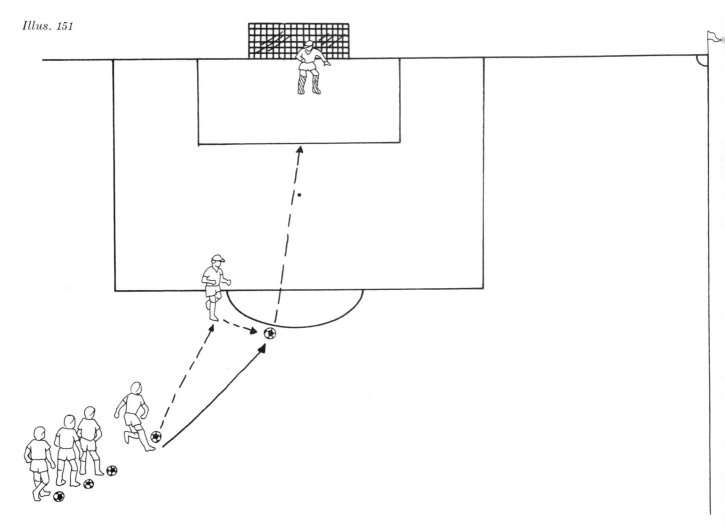

96

Illus. 152. One-on-one, going to goal inside the penalty box. Concentrate on getting the shot off quickly.

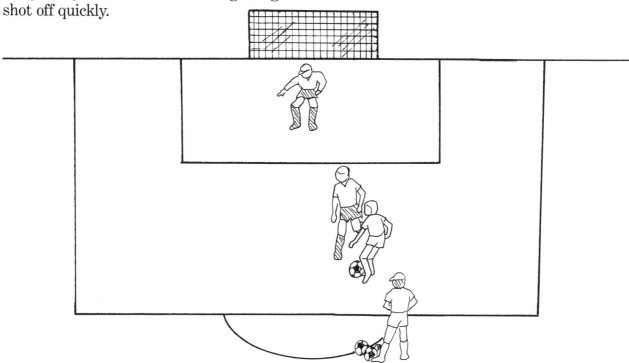

Illus. 153. Use an extended penalty box, playing two-on-two, three-on-three, and four-on-four. In this practice work on combination play resulting in getting a shot on goal.

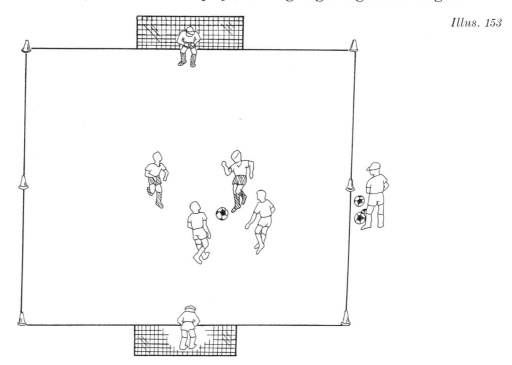

VIII   Crosses

A good defending team tries to keep the attacking team from penetrating their defense—pushing them to the outside, or the flank, in the attacking third of the field. Because defenses put so many players in their goal area, the flanks have the most time and space for the attacking team to penetrate in the attacking third. This also allows the ball to be crossed from the flanker into the penalty box for strikes on goal. There are three primary targets which the attacking team tries to find: the near post, the middle of the goal, and the far post.

The Near Post Cross

The target area which the server tries to find is on the edge of the six yard box, even with or slightly ahead of the near post. Before the server crosses the ball he must take three elements into consideration: space available, position of defending players, and position of attacking players.

Illus. 154. Make sure space is available at the near post. An attacking player does not want to stand in the near post space. He should wait until the last possible second before sprinting into this space to strike.

Illus. 154

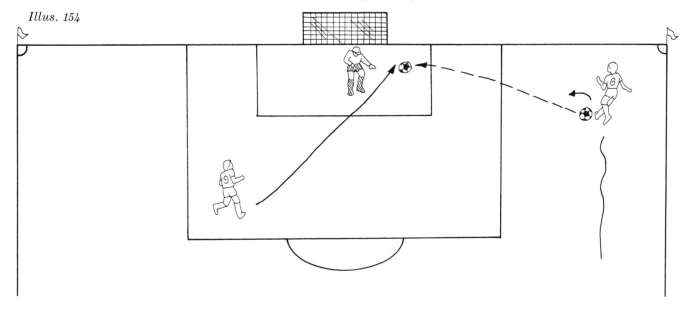

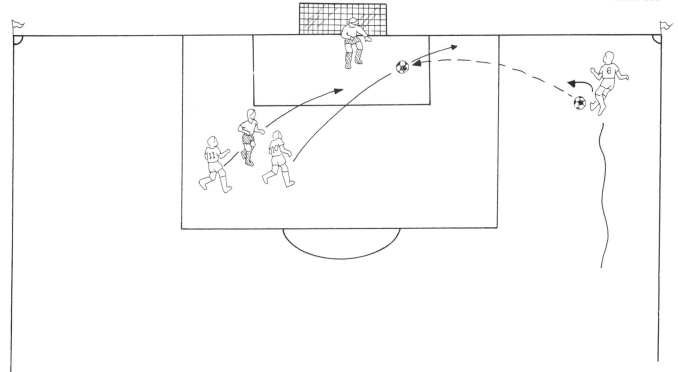

Illus. 155. If for some reason the attacking player runs into this space too early and does not receive the cross, he must continue his run and get out of this space so that it will open up again.

Illus. 156. The player can also back out of the near post space. This creates the space again. He can then run back into the space when the time is right with the timing of the cross.

Illus. 156

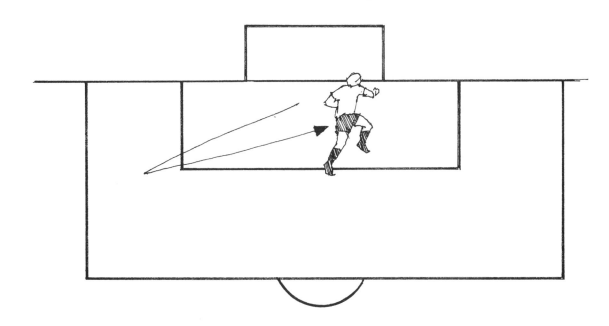

Illus. 157. When the server is galloping down the touch line, he must be able to look up and see where the defending players are, including the goalkeeper. The closer the crosser takes the ball to the goal line, the closer the goalkeeper will drift towards the near post. This makes the near post even more difficult to score from.

Illus. 158. It is best for the ball and the near post runner to arrive in the near post space at the same time. This leaves space in front of the runner, giving him room to operate.

Illus. 157

Illus. 158

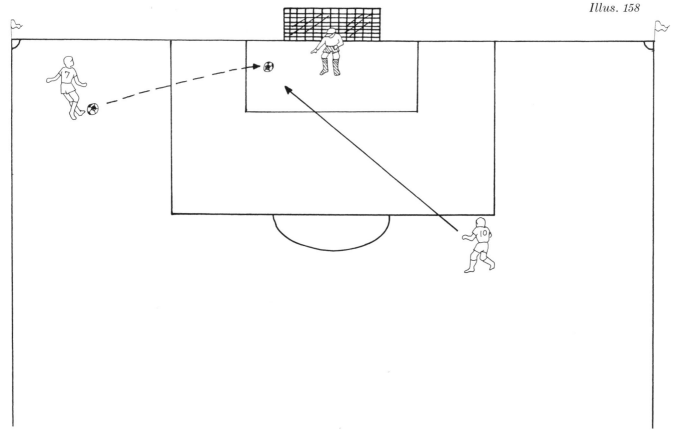

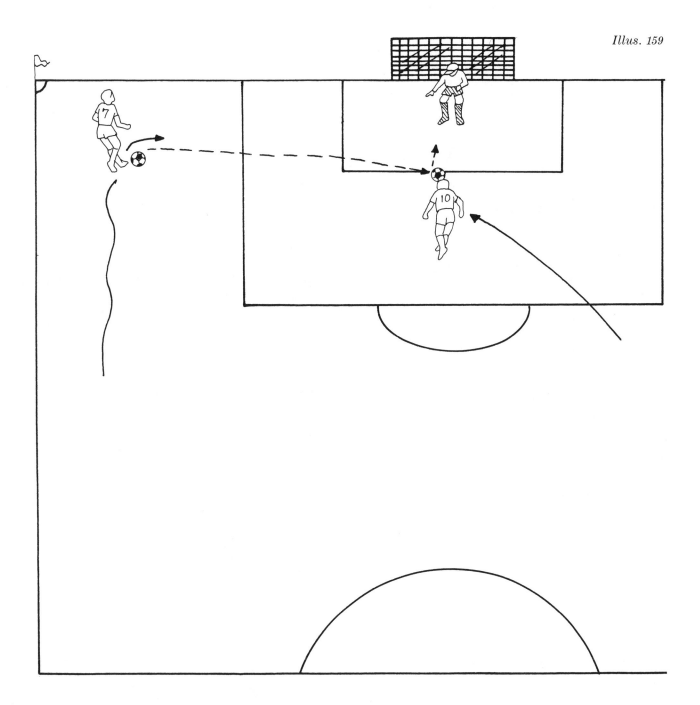

Illus. 159. The cross should be taken as far as possible down the touch line and driven hard back at an angle behind the defense. When crossing the ball to the near post, drive the ball hard. This makes it easier for the attacking players to redirect the ball on to goal or to flick the ball on for attacking players behind them. With the ball being driven, all it has to do is hit an attacking or defending player and deflect into the goal. The driven ball is much harder for goalkeepers to handle and for defenders to clear. If penetration down the touch line is limited, a hard bending ball into the near post is required.

Illus. 160

Illus. 161

Illus. 162

Illus. 160–164. On the last touch before the attacking player crosses the ball, the server can push the ball straight down the touch line, so when he is ready to cross the ball he can plant his foot towards the goal and turn his body to cross the ball. However, this is very hard, especially running at full speed under pressure. It is not recommended for younger players. A problem occurs when the player does not get all the way around the ball

Illus. 163

Illus. 164

Illus. 165

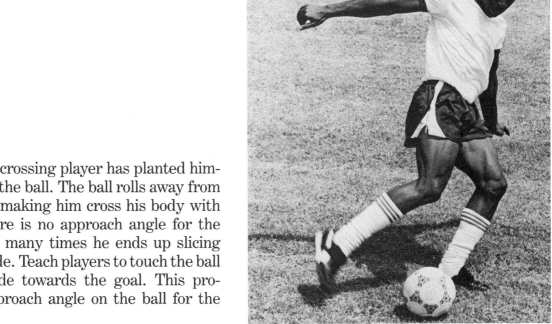

because the crossing player has planted himself to cross the ball. The ball rolls away from the crosser, making him cross his body with his leg. There is no approach angle for the crosser, and many times he ends up slicing the cross wide. Teach players to touch the ball slightly inside towards the goal. This provides an approach angle on the ball for the crosser.

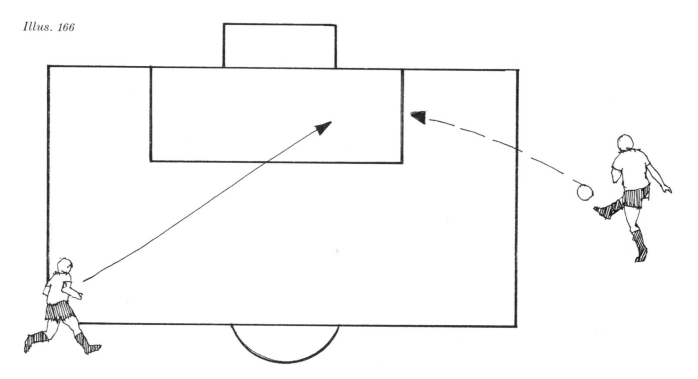

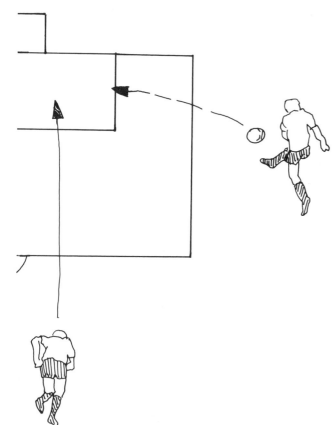

Illus. 166. Players running to the near post should do so at a 40° angle to have the best chance of making good body contact with the ball. Many times a young player will run straight at the near post. This provides no angle of attack.

Illus. 167. The near post runner should time his run so that he comes late, but at speed. If he gets into the space too early, he'll be caught waiting on the ball. Direct the ball in a downward path to the goal at contact. The near post runner can also flick the ball on to the players behind him, although this is not always possible. The near post runner is primarily trying to redirect the cross into the goal. The speed of the runner and the speed of the cross will be enough to beat the goalkeeper.

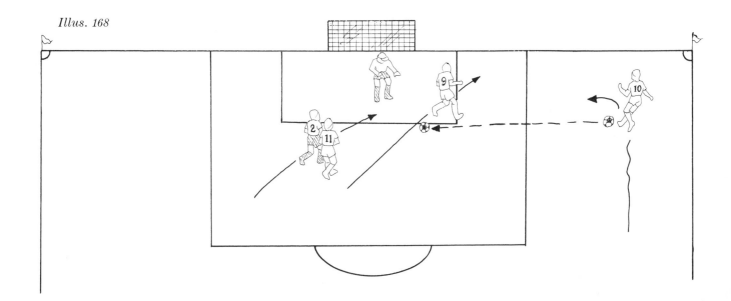

Illus. 168. A third option is to step over the ball or dummy the ball and let it run across the front of the goal.

Practice:

Have players line up on the touch line, first stationary; then serving the ball into the near post. Have the server serve the ball at running speed. Have the other players make their runs to the near post. After some proficiency has been achieved, put a defender on the near post runner *(Illus. 169).*

Illus. 169

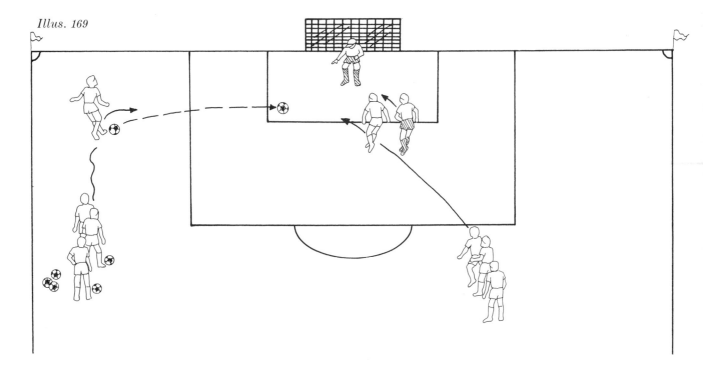

Middle of the Goal Crosses

The target area for the middle of the goal cross is around the penalty spot. If the cross is too far to the inside of the penalty spot the goalkeeper should be able to win possession of the ball. The problem in this cross is finding time and space in that area of the penalty box.

Illus. 170. One way to create time and space is to drag marking defenders beyond the near post. The problem in modern soccer is that teams are now defending with so many players that the attacking team may have to send more than one runner to the near post.

Illus. 170

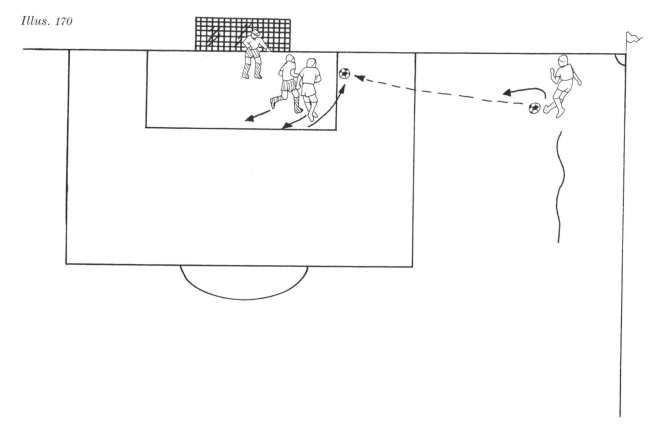

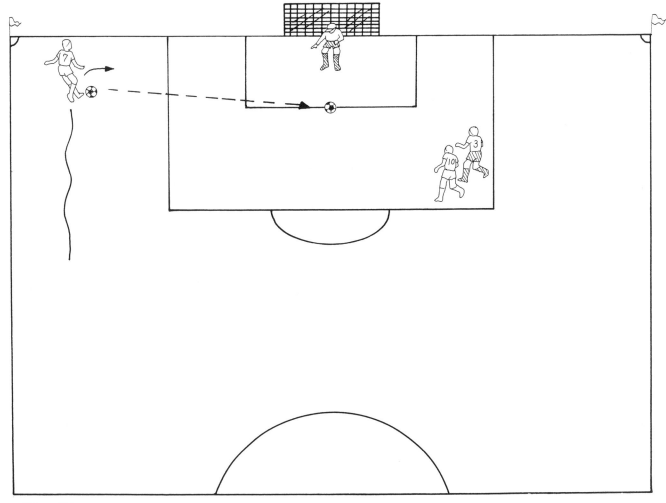

Illus. 171

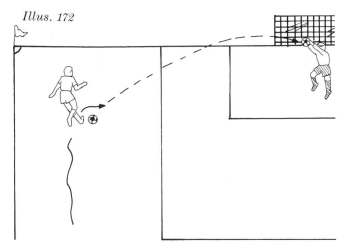

Illus. 172

Illus. 171. Another way to create time and space is to keep defenders away from the target area. This can be done by avoiding the target area until the last possible moment.

Illus. 172. A third way is if the attacking player can start his run in the target area and make a run to the far post, dragging the defender out of the target area space, creating the space for the attacking player to run back into.

The middle of the goal is not the best target area for crosses. This cross does not really take any defenders out of the game because the ball stays in front of most of them. Realistically, the goalkeeper should win possession on most crosses to this area.

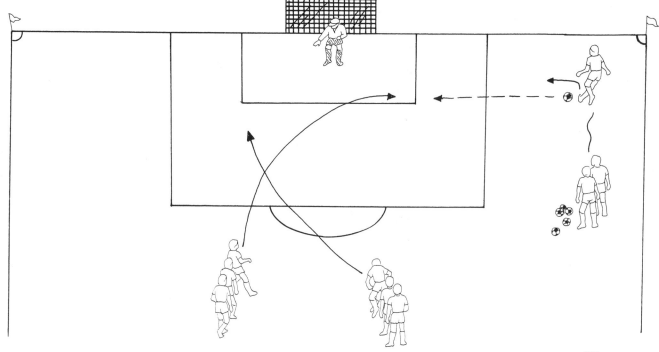

Illus. 173

Practice:

Have players out on the touch line, but not always serving from the same place. This will cross balls in the middle of the goal area with two players trying to score goals. Add defenders to make the task more realistic. Make sure the server serves from different areas of the field *(Illus. 173).*

Coaching Points for Middle of the Goal Runner

• Angle of the run.
• Timing of the run.
• Not getting caught in the space.
• Hitting the target.

Coaching Points for the Crosser

• Head up so that the crosser can identify the target area, the attacking player and the defending player.
• Proper last touch on the ball before crossing the ball.
• Proper cross flight.

Far Post Crosses

The actual target area here is behind the far post. The depth of the cross will largely depend on the position of the goalkeeper. The server and the far post runner should be aware of their positions and make their runs accordingly.

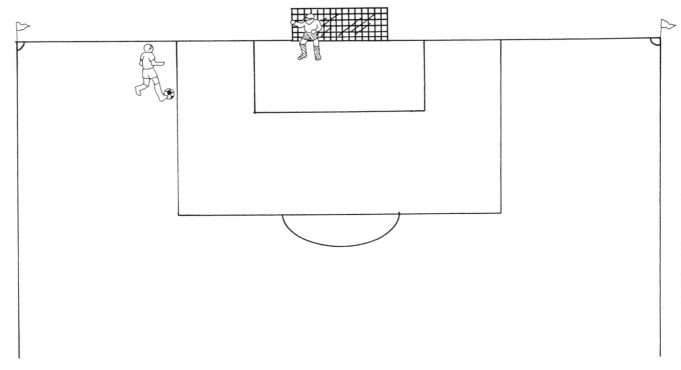

Illus. 174

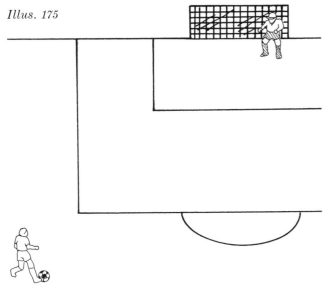

Illus. 175

Illus. 174. If the server is 20 or 30 yards from the goal, the goalkeeper will shade towards the near post. Lift the ball enough to go over the defenders into the space behind them.

Illus. 175. If the server is farther out on the touch line, the goalkeeper will shade to his far post, making the cross beyond the six yard box. Not many goals will be scored directly from this cross, so head or volley the ball back across the face of the goal *(Illus. 176)*. In this type of cross, play the ball behind the defenders, who must now turn and react. As the ball plays back across the face of the goal, the defender must again turn and react. Because the defender must turn to find the ball, the possibility of the attacking player losing his marker is even greater.

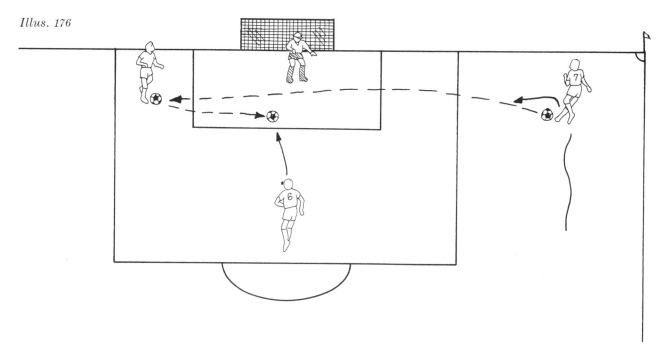

Illus. 177. The run to the far post is a wide, bent run. Do not turn one's back to the server or the goal. The runner should arrive late and at speed, making a wide bent run so that the cross is not played over his head. If he sees that the ball is going over his head, he can backtrack to recover the ball. When the run is bent, he can react easier going forward than backwards, and he can see the whole field.

Illus. 177

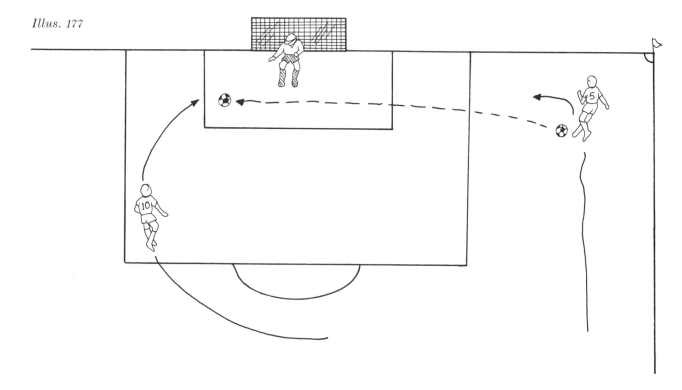

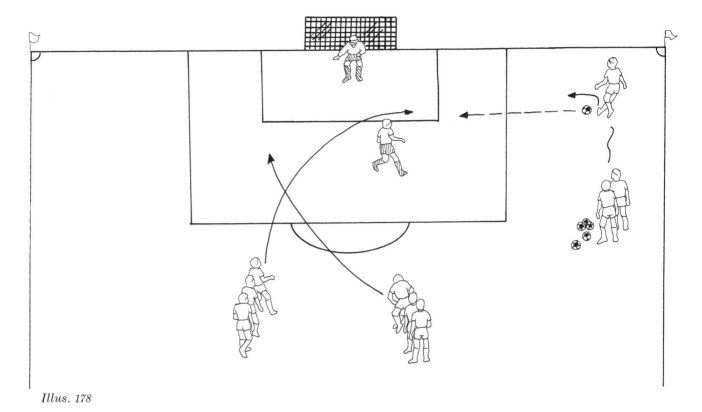

Illus. 178

Practice:

Have servers out on the touch line serving to the back post, trying to score, or volleying balls back across the face of the goal *(Illus. 178)*.

───── **Coaching Points for the Crosser** ─────

• Head up so that the crosser can identify the target area, attacking player, defending player, and the proper flighted ball.

───── **Coaching Points for the Runner** ─────

• Angle of run.
• Turning of the run.
• Being first to the ball.
• Hit the goal.
• Head or volley back across the face of the goal.

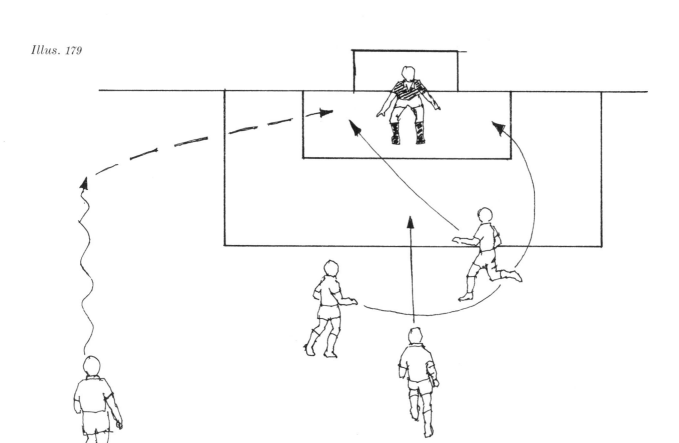

Practice:

Have two serving lines with runners coming to the near post, the far post and the middle of the goal area. Alternate sides, and make sure the near post runner goes first with the far post running off his run, followed by the marker or the runner going to the middle of the goal area *(Illus. 179)*.

—— Coaching Points for the Crosser ——

• Head up to identify the target area, defending players, and attacking players.
• Last touch before the cross.
• Proper service.

—— Coaching Points for the Runner ——

• Near post runner goes first; far post second.
• Angle of the runner.
• Timing of the runner.
• Being first to the ball.
• Hitting the goal.

IX Goalkeeping

A goalkeeper's motto should always be "safety first." One way to achieve this is to get his body behind the ball whenever possible. This presents two barriers to the incoming ball: the goalkeeper's hands and body. Many times a goalkeeper gets lazy and doesn't position his body behind the ball; then reaches or even dives for the ball, when instead all he has to do is move his feet and get behind the ball. Poor positioning turns an easy save into a hard save and increases the chance for a mistake.

Illus. 180. The position of the goalkeeper's hands should take the form of a "W" or be identical to the shape of taking a throw-in. After making this shape, the goalkeeper should stick his fingertips out to help take the shock of the catch and present a soft surface. If the goalkeeper's palms are sticking out, a hard surface will be presented, making a catch difficult.

Illus. 180

Catching Low Balls

There are two primary methods of catching a rolling or bouncing ball: *Illus. 181–183.* Catching the ball with feet together . . . *Illus. 184–186* . . . or catching the ball while kneeling.

Illus. 181

Illus. 182

Illus. 183

Illus. 184

Illus. 185

Illus. 186

Practice:

Roll and bounce balls to a stationary goalkeeper so that he can practice each of the two techniques; then serve soccer balls where he has to move to get into position to perform these techniques.

— Coaching Points for the Goalkeeper —

- Identify the path of the ball early.
- Get the body behind the ball.
- Present the hands in an open fashion so that the ball will roll into his hands and be curled up into the forearms and chest.
- Keep legs together so that the ball does not go through them.
- Keep his eyes on the ball.

Catching Medium High Balls

There are two primary methods for catching the medium high ball: the hands-out method, and the hands-under method.

Illus. 187–188. In the hands-out method the goalkeeper extends his hands, forming a "W" shape and bending his elbows to absorb the shock.

Illus. 187

Illus. 188

Illus. 189–191. In the hands-under method the goalkeeper uses his hands to trap the ball against his body, and wrap the ball up into his chest with his forearms.

Illus. 189

Illus. 190

Illus. 191

Practice:

Throw or kick a half-volley ball to a stationary goalkeeper. After introducing the two methods, repeat the service while making the goalkeeper move into position; then have the goalkeeper stand facing the goal. On a verbal command have him turn and take the service from a player or coach who is shooting on goal.

Coaching Points

- Identify the path of the ball early.
- Get one's body behind the ball.
- Decide how to receive the shot.
- Keep eyes on the ball.

Catching High Balls

Judgment is very important when catching high balls. If the goalkeeper comes out either too early or too late, a goal will result. This can only improve through practise.

Once the flight of the ball is identified, the goalkeeper should come late but fast and in one fluid motion. This will enable the goalkeeper to collect the ball at its highest point before the attackers can get to it. If the goalkeeper comes out, stops and *then* tries to go forward, an opposing player can get in the path of the ball. This loss of momentum will not allow the goalkeeper to get the ball at its highest point.

The goalkeeper should always announce his presence by calling for the ball. This alerts his teammates that he is coming out, and the communication can intimidate attackers.

Illus. 192–194. The mechanics of this move are as follows: Using a one-footed take-off, bring one knee up to the chest with the arms following through. This gets the goalkeeper to his highest point. Fully extend the arms with the hands forming the "W" shape. Once the catch is made, he should bring the ball to his chest for safety.

Illus. 192

Practice:

Have a person throw high balls to a goalkeeper who must take the air ball; then add an attacker who will contest for the ball. Use hand service. When proficiency is achieved, have player cross balls into the penalty box for the goalkeeper to handle. Add attackers to make the practice more realistic.

Illus. 193   *Illus. 194*

Punching the Ball

Illus. 195–197. Sometimes when the ball crosses into the penalty box, the goalkeeper is not sure if he can catch it. Remembering "safety first," the goalkeeper will come out and punch the ball out of danger. The mechanics of punching the ball are much the same as catching crosses, except that the goalkeeper comes out and applies a two-handed punch. Some goalkeepers use a one-handed punch, but this creates a greater chance of a mistake because of the smaller surface. The punch should propel the ball high, far and wide, giving the goalkeeper and his teammates the time to reorganize.

Practice:

Have crossers and shooters outside the penalty box. Give each one a number for the coach to call out. At first the goalkeeper will be in the penalty box by himself and will handle crosses and shooters; then add attackers to put pressure on the goalkeeper on crosses and to deflect shooters on goal.

Coaching Points

- Identify the flight of the ball.
- Keep eyes on the ball.
- Come late but at speed.
- Announce your presence.
- Bring arms and knees through.
- Punch ball at highest point.

Illus. 195

Illus. 196

Illus. 197

Power Diving

The power dive is used to make saves on shots when the goalkeeper cannot merely move over and save the shot.

Illus. 198–200. The most important element in power diving is the footwork. The footwork allows the goalkeeper to get into position to make the save. If the footwork is not there, the goalkeeper will never make the save.

Illus. 198

Illus. 199

Illus. 200

Illus. 200A

Illus. 200A. A common fault of a young goalkeeper is crossing his legs. When he does this, he will be off balance and unable to recover. The footwork should be a shuffle or side-to-side.

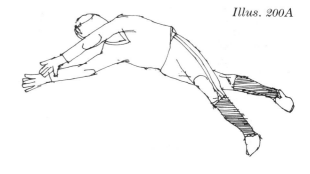

One of the hardest parts of goalkeeping is getting over the fear of landing on the hard ground. Using a mat or some other soft surface in practice may help.

Practice:

Have the goalkeeper dive for the ball on a soft surface. Use hand service, and pay attention to footwork; then have the goalkeeper dive over human ponies. Make sure to use hand service. After having the goalkeeper practise power diving over the human ponies, have the goalkeeper take proper shots on goal. Re-member to emphasize the proper footwork (*Illus. 201–204*).

Coaching Points

- Identify the flight of the ball.
- Proper footwork.
- Eyes on the ball.
- Decide to catch or flick away.
- If catch, form "W" shape.
- If catch, land on the ball.
- If flick away, get up and move quickly back into position.

Illus. 201

Illus. 202

Illus. 203

Illus. 204

Deflecting the Ball Over the Bar

Illus. 205. Again remembering safety first, deflect the ball over the bar. This works well when the goalkeeper has been caught off the line too far.

Illus. 206. The goalkeeper must turn his body and use a cross over step to get back to tip the ball over.

Illus. 207. If the goalkeeper turns to his left he should use his right hand to do the tipping, and vice versa. The goalkeeper should use his fingertips to guide the ball over the bar.

Practice:

Have the goalkeeper perform the tipping technique without the ball, or have him mimic it. When this is done, start the goalkeeper out

Illus. 205

Illus. 206

Illus. 207

of his goal and hand-serve him the ball to tip over the bar; then start the goalkeeper out of his goal with a simple push pass, so he can make the save. The goalkeeper returns the ball to the server with the server knocking a ball over the goalkeeper's head. The goalkeeper must turn and tip the ball over the bar. Repeat the process.

Coaching Points

- Identify the flight of the ball.
- Turn and get back quickly.
- Use proper hand.
- Jump off back foot.
- Use fingertips.

Illus. 208

Goalkeeper Distribution

The goalkeeper is the last line of defense *and* the first line of offense. He starts the attack by properly choosing the method of distribution—rolling the ball out, throwing it out, or kicking it out.

Rolling the Ball Out

Illus. 208. Rolling the ball out is a very accurate way to pass it to a teammate. The goalkeeper steps to his target and rolls the ball with his hand touching the top of the grass. The goalkeeper should get low enough and not bounce the ball into the ground to make handling easier. Make sure there is a follow-through with the pass ending up at a teammate's feet.

Throwing the Ball Out

Illus. 209–211. This technique covers over much greater distance, up to 40 or 50 yards. The goalkeeper steps to his target and uses an over-the-head roundhouse throw, hand cupping the ball.

Make sure the pass is on a straight line, *not* an arch. An arch puts the ball in the air longer, giving more time for defenders to get to the receiver and apply pressure to him. The goalkeepers must try at all costs to get the pass waist high through the air to his teammates. If the ball is thrown short, the field becomes a factor and the ball becomes much harder to judge and handle, especially if the throw-in is short hopped.

Illus. 209

Illus. 210

Illus. 211

Kicking the Ball Out

There are three ways to kick the ball out: the goal kick, the punt, and the half volley.

Illus. 212. When using a goal kick, use a full instep drive to obtain maximum length.

Illus. 212

Illus. 213

Illus. 214

Illus. 213. When punting the ball out, the goalkeeper is looking for length and accuracy. Punting a soccer ball is much like punting a football. The ball should be dropped and not thrown up in the air, since it creates much greater room for error (the wind may blow the ball down, or the goalkeeper may hit it too high).

Illus. 214. After the goalkeeper drops the ball he should make contact with it between his knees and his waist. This ensures that the ball will not be kicked either too high or too low.

Illus. 215. The goalkeeper should not take his eyes off the ball while it travels down and hits his foot, and should strike it with his instep, keeping his foot pointed, with proper follow-through.

Illus. 216

Illus. 217

Illus. 216. The third method a goalkeeper can use is a half volley. This kick ensures a long and low trajectory. It is easier to receive, even head-on.

Illus. 217. However, there are disadvantages, such as uneven ground causing the ball to bounce erratically. To avoid this, the goalkeeper *must* keep his eyes on the ball while hitting it with his instep.

X   Defending Set Pieces

It is commonly quoted that 40 to 60% of all goals are scored from set pieces. If this is the case, why is it so difficult to defend them?

Illus. 218. Organization: An organized team can put pressure on the opponents by placing large numbers of defending players in pre-planned areas of the field, while there is a general lack of defensive organization and even panic at set pieces. The attacking team knows what is coming, and the defending team is reacting to the set piece.

Illus. 218

Illus. 219

Illus. 219. Discipline: The set piece depends on each player's performance to be successful. If a player forgets or even reacts slowly, his performance may lead to his team giving up a goal.

Illus. 220. Concentration: Goals are scored on set pieces because many players view a set piece as a chance to relax. Relaxing, however, causes players to lose concentration. Players can also lose concentration when they retreat with their backs to the ball. Defending players must concentrate on marking attacking players as well as dangerous space. This may require the defending team to bring every one of their players back to defend.

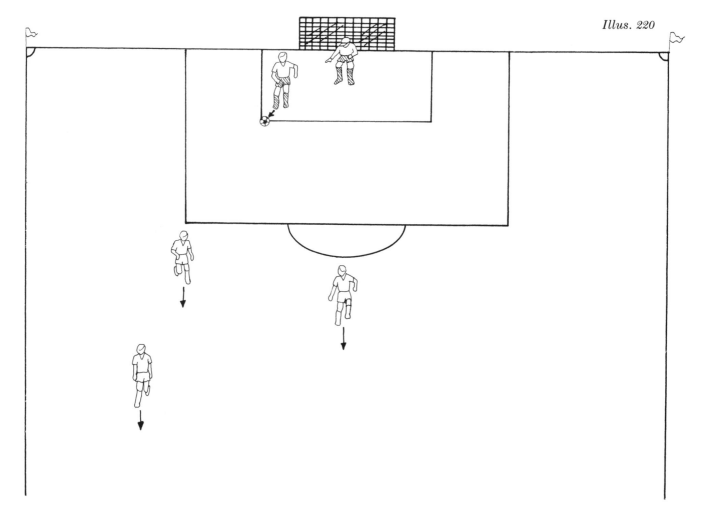

Illus. 220

Defending Free Kicks in the Middle Third of the Field

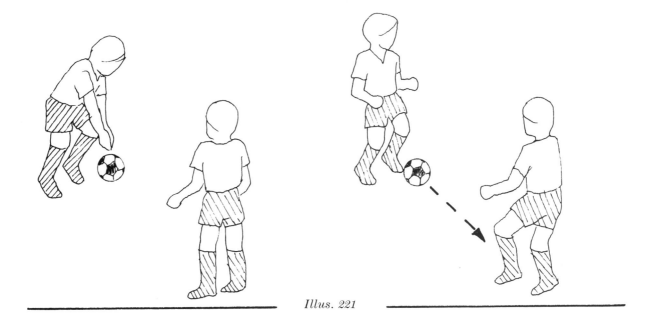

Illus. 221

Illus. 221. When a free kick is awarded in the middle third of the field, most attacking teams will try to put the ball down quickly and play quickly, trying to exploit any tactical and concentration breakdown by the defending team. The attacking team will also try to exploit the space which is awarded to them.

Illus. 222. The defending team can stop this quick free kick by moving into position 10 yards from the ball. Now the attacking team must pass the ball in a path of less penetration, requiring them to use a more difficult technique of service, which could make the receiver's job of getting the ball under control and starting the attack even harder. Slowing down the quick free kick will also allow teammates to get organized and mark attacking players as well as dangerous space.

Setting the Wall

When a free kick is given around the box or an indirect free kick is given inside the box, the defending team must quickly organize and set up a defensive wall to help block the direct shot on goal. This is done by solving four major problems.

Illus. 223. Lining Up the Wall. When a free kick is given around the box, the goalkeeper usually tries to line the wall up instead of covering the whole goal. This exposes the goal to the quick shot. Lining up the wall should be done by a predetermined field player, standing behind the ball facing the goal. This done, the goalkeeper can prepare for a quick shot on goal and not worry about setting up the wall. The goalkeeper's position should be such that he can see the ball, not get caught behind the wall, and try at all times to be near the center of the goal.

Illus. 223

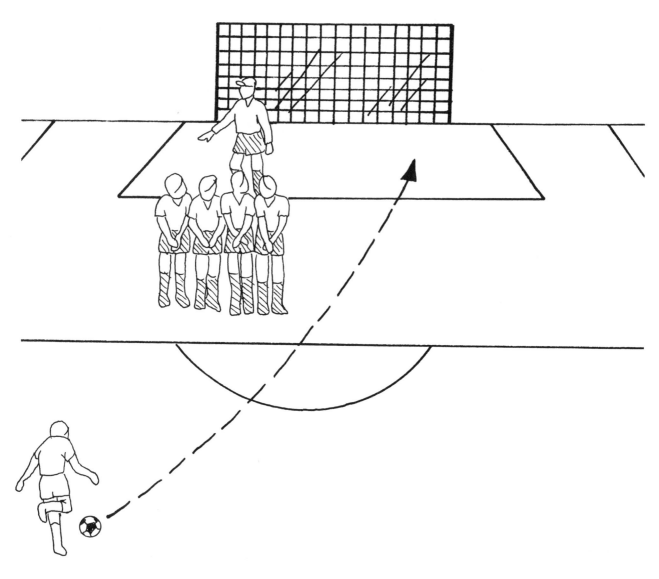

Illus. 224–226. Putting Players in the Wall. The placement of the free kick will determine how many players to put in the wall. If the defending team puts too many players in the wall, they will be at a numerical disadvantage, and the goalkeeper's vision will be blocked. For the goalkeeper to be able to see the ball, he must move laterally away from the wall. This will push him away from the middle of the goal and expose him to bending both over and around the wall.

There are three golden rules to remember:
• If the free kick is in the "D", the wall should have 4 to 5 players *(Illus. 224)*.
• If the free kick is from the "D" to the corner of the box, there should be 3–4 players *(Illus. 225)*.
• If the free kick is from the corner of the penalty box to the touch line, there should be 2 players *(Illus. 226)*.

Illus. 224

Illus. 225

Illus. 226

Remember that the number of players in the wall will differ because of the position of the ball. As the ball moves away from the goal towards the touch line, fewer numbers will be required in the wall. Consider also the opponent's ability to bend the ball over and around the wall.

Illus. 227. Lining Up the Wall Players. When planning defensive walls, predetermine who will go into the wall. In doing so, keep in mind that the player on the outside of the wall should overlap the outside post. This will help prevent the ball from being bent around the outside of the wall. Remember, also, that players who are positioned in the wall should line up by height, tallest on the outside and shortest on the inside. These players must stay close together, with their feet tight, so that shots on goal cannot get there. Finally, never let attacking players get in the wall. If a player should move out of the wall, his absence will leave a hole where the attacking team can shoot through.

Illus. 228. When to Break the Wall. The wall must not break until after the ball has been kicked, otherwise the attacking team will have large holes towards the unprotected goal. If the wall does move, it should move as a unit towards the ball just as it is being kicked. This decreases the angle for the shooter.

In the 1986 World Cup in Mexico, a tactic that the West Germans used was to all jump straight up in the air to increase the height of the wall just as the ball was going to be kicked.

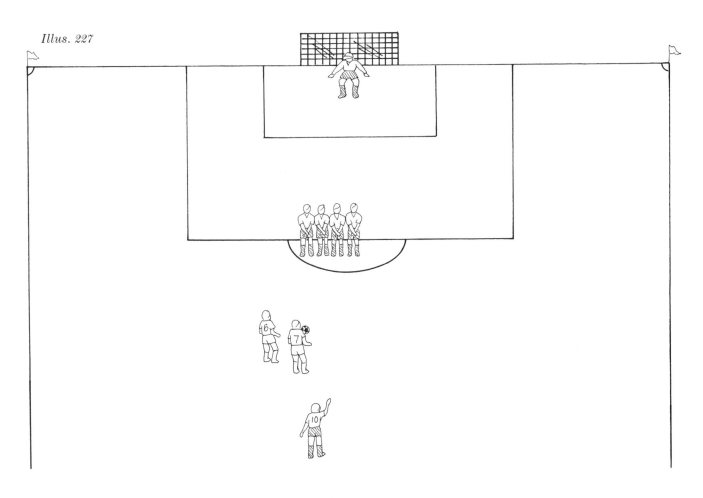

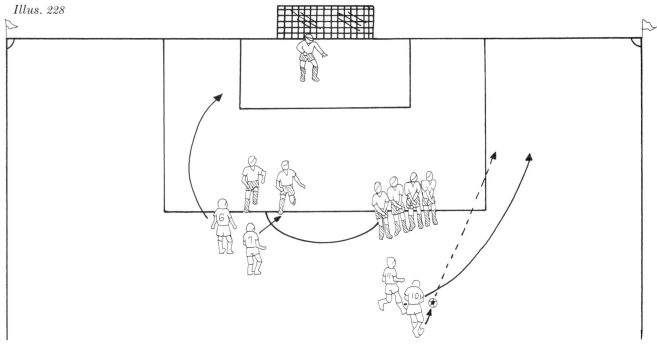

Indirect Free Kicks Inside the Penalty Area

An indirect free kick inside the penalty area is not that frequent an occurrence because it must touch another player before a goal can be scored. If the ball is in a good shooting position, do the following:

Illus. 229. If the 10-yard rule is in effect, a team will have to build an 11-man human wall on the goal line with the goalkeeper in front of the wall. As soon as the ball is touched, have the goalkeeper charge the ball or use a "kamikaze" player to rush the ball, with the goalkeeper staying put. Some coaches send the whole wall as soon as the ball has been played. However, after taking the kick and before making the second touch, the wall must come out and close down the ball.

Illus. 229

Corner Kicks

In one way, defending corners is like defending free kicks—there should be a player assigned to disturb the service of the corner if possible.

Illus. 230. The position of this defending player will depend on whether the corner is an outswinger or an inswinger. If the corner is going to be an outswinger, the defending player will position himself close to the goalline. If the corner is an inswinger, the defending player should be farther out from the goal line.

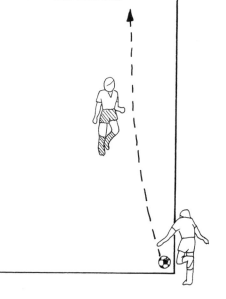

Illus. 230

I always tell my players to line up with the ball to make the service go between the defending player and the goal line. This creates pressure because the attackers are playing the ball into a small area which will increase the percentage of error. It will also help the defending players in the box and the goalkeeper to judge where the service will be coming into the box, because it forces the ball higher and wider from the goal.

Illus. 231. If the attacking team tries to play a short corner, the defending team must send out two players (three would be even better). If not, the attacking team will have a two-on-one situation which is not acceptable in any defending situation.

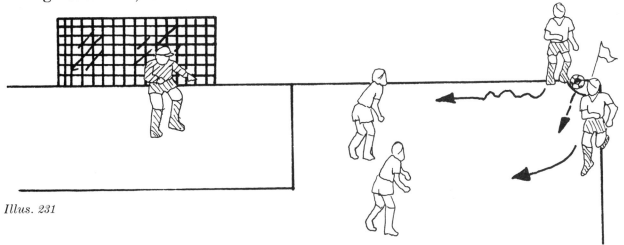

Illus. 231

Goalkeeper Position

When a team is defending a corner kick, the goalkeeper in the box directs his defending team. However, he must also start the whole process by positioning himself correctly.

Illus. 232. The major threat from the corner is an inswing to the front half of the goal.

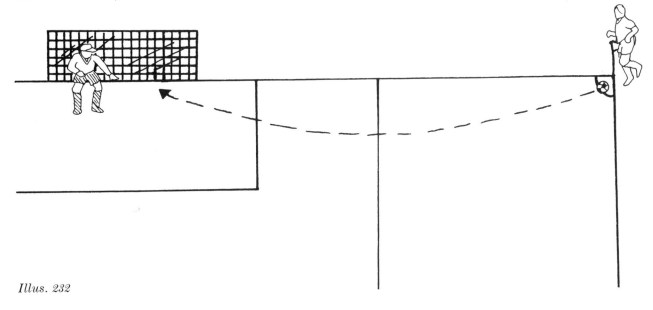

Illus. 232

Illus. 233. If the goalkeeper positions himself too far from the far post, he runs the high risk of simply not getting to the ball first. He also may have his path obstructed by both defending and attacking players. The best position for the goalkeeper is halfway in his goal. He should also face out in a sideways position, feet out. This way he has the best possible view of the whole field, and is in a much better position to backtrack to balls which are played over his head.

Illus. 233

Defending the Far Post

Illus. 234. The player defending the far post should be like the goalkeeper, facing out but inside the far post.

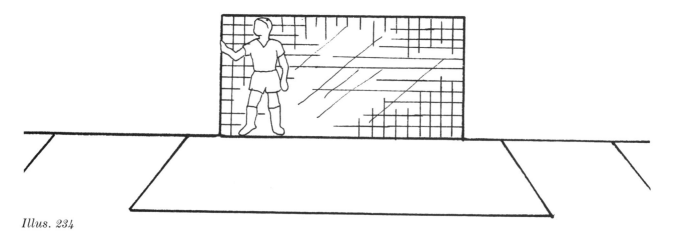

Illus. 234

Defending the Near Post

Illus. 235. The player who is defending the near post should position himself so that he is overlapping the near post. This is done so balls don't squeeze in between the defending player and the near post. If the goalkeeper comes off his line to make a save, the two players on the post should come off the post and help cover the goal.

The rest of the marking can be done either by man to man or by zone.

Illus. 235

Illus. 236

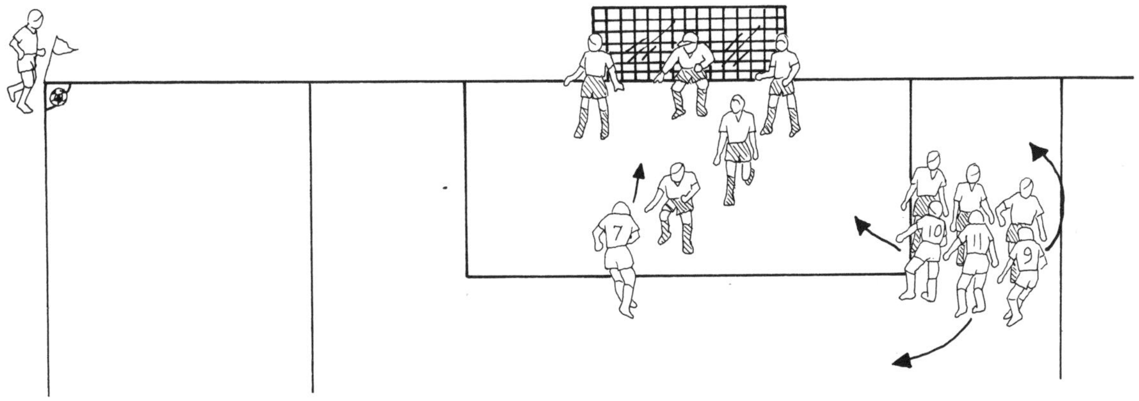

Illus. 236. When the defending team is marking man for man, each marking player is responsible for his players until the ball has been cleared or won by the goalkeeper. There should also be a free player whose job is to key on the ball and go win it. This player's only marking responsibility is the ball.

Illus. 237. When using a zone to mark on corners, each player has an area for which he is responsible for anything entering in front of him or his zone. The defending player's zone is all in front of him, not behind him. In this defensive scheme the player must guard his area very aggressively.

Illus. 237

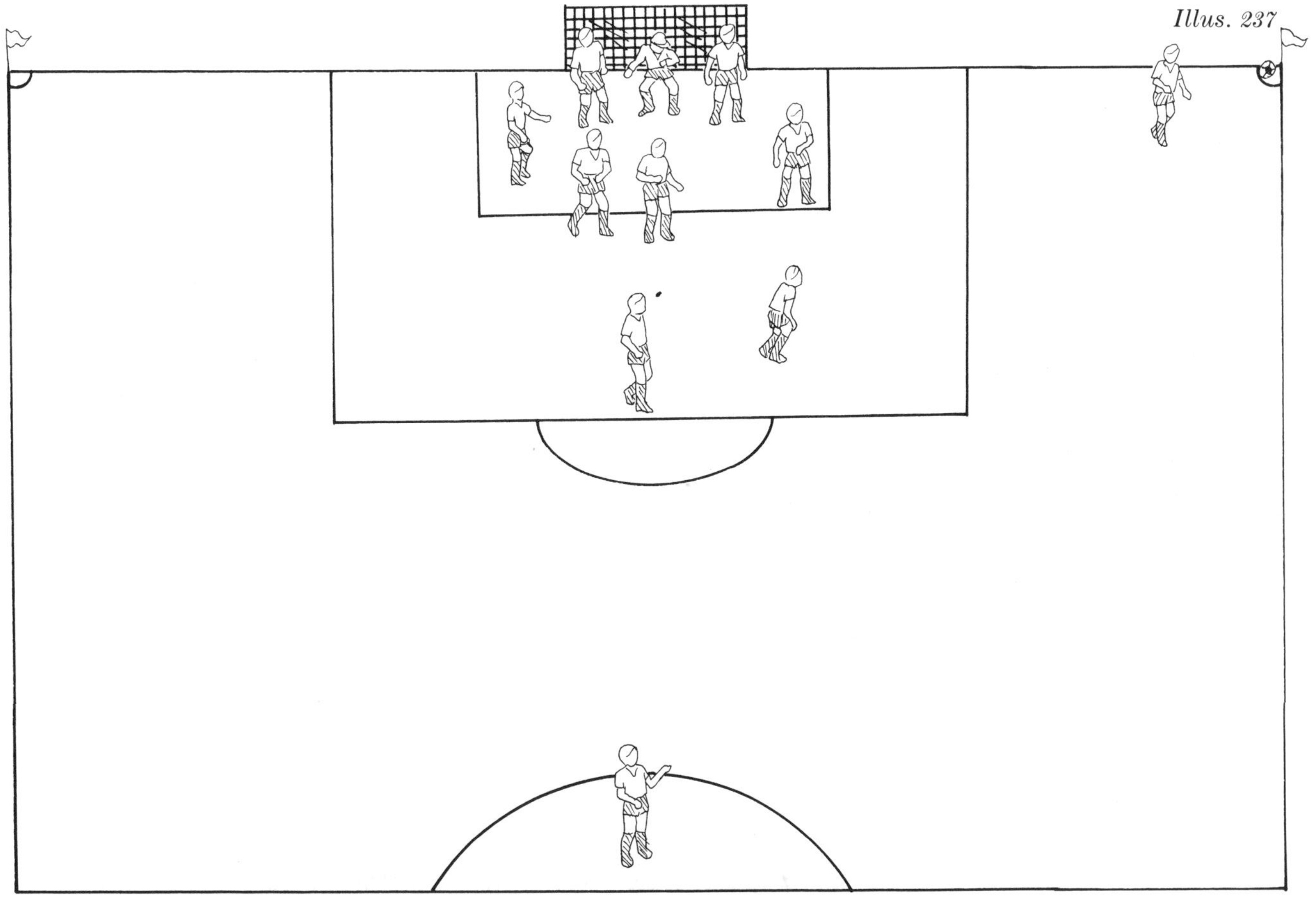

Defending Throw-ins

Illus. 238. When defending on normal throw-ins, players should do four things: keep concentration; move into marking position while the ball is out of play; mark tight in the area of the throw, including the thrower, making sure not to lose the marker if he goes on a run; and apply pressure to the player the thrower plays to. This makes his first touch even harder to control.

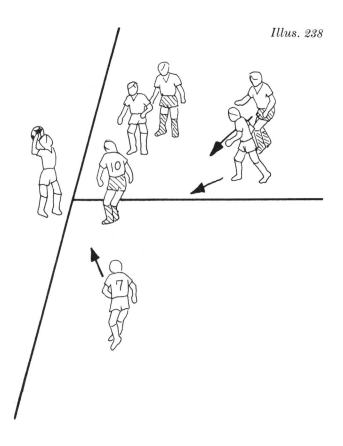

Illus. 239. When defending long throw-ins in the defending third of the field: the goalkeeper should position himself towards the front half of the goal; players should mark behind the player who is receiving the throw, keeping the goalkeeper and other defending players aware of the flick going off the target player; mark the space in front of the target player; mark all runners who are running off the target player to keep them from getting the flick on; and, depending on the thrower, have a defending player go and stand in front of him. This will reduce the distance of the throw.

Illus. 239

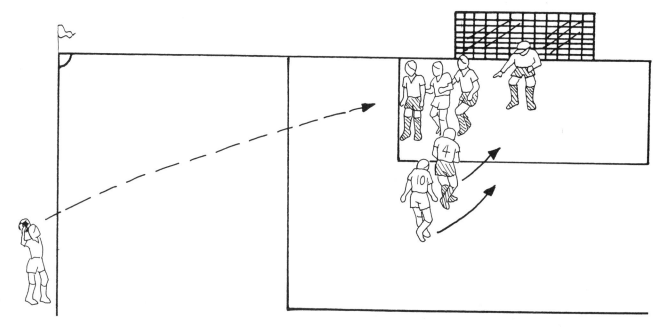

140

XI   Attacking Set Pieces

Set Pieces in the Midfield Area

Illus. 240

Illus. 240. When the attacking team has a free kick in midfield, they should take it quickly and continue the attacking move. Free kicks tend to make the defending team lose concentration. Some players may even turn their backs to the ball. A quick free kick takes advantage of these defensive mistakes.

Illus. 241. Play the free kick to the player closest to the ball. Now comes the dangerous part, because the player who takes the free kick will be concentrating on finding the closest player so that he can play the ball to him.

This second player should be looking around to play a penetrating pass that will elude the most defenders as well as keep the attacking move going and keep possession.

Illus. 241

Illus. 242. While this is going on in midfield, the forward players should be looking for any opportunity to get behind the defending team player to receive a pass.

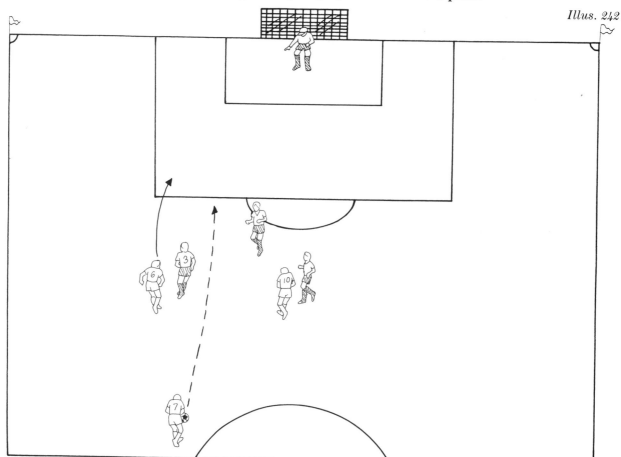

Attacking Throw-Ins

At any level of soccer, there will be more attacking throw-ins than any other type of set piece. During these throw-ins, the defending players tend to relax and lose their concentration, because although throw-ins look harmless, they can be very dangerous in the attacking third of the field. Remember four points:

Illus. 243. Take the throw-in as quickly as possible, but at the same time, stay in control and make the right tactical decision. At any level, defenders losing their concentration during throw-ins should be punished.

Illus. 243

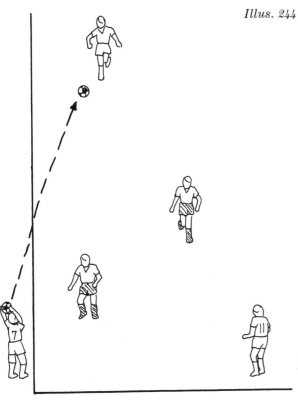

Illus. 244. Always look for the farthest unmarked player when taking a throw-in. Remember one can be in an offside position and receive the ball directly from the thrower without being offside. If this option is not available, throw in the ball to the nearest unmarked player—he will have time and space to play the ball back to the thrower or to initiate the next attack himself. The most important thing is to keep possession of the ball.

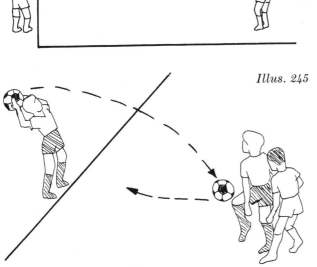

Illus. 245. Make the throw-in easy for the receiver to control as well as one touch playable, if possible. All age players have a tendency to throw the ball short. With so many games being played on very hard and uneven surfaces, the receiver does not really know how or where the ball will bounce. Because of this, the ball dictates to the player, instead of the player dictating to the ball. Astroturf® is another consideration. On Astroturf® the ball will skip or run away from the player who is receiving the throw-in. Try to throw the ball where the receiver controls the ball out of the air, or plays it back to the thrower in the air. Also, when a difficult throw-in is taken, it kills the time and space of the receiver which may result in loss of possession. So throwing the ball where it is easy to control is very important.

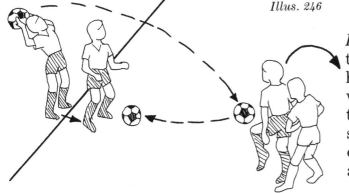

Illus. 246. The thrower must get back into the game as quickly as possible. This makes him available if the receiver of the throw-in wants to play the ball directly back to the thrower. If this is not possible, the thrower should support his teammates in possession of the ball and create attacking numbers up around the ball.

The Long Throw-In

The long throw-in is a very dangerous and effective attacking weapon. It is dangerous because the ball is played to a predetermined target area on the field; it is accurate because it is being served by hands and not feet, and the thrower is not restricted by any defender.

Illus. 247. The thrower must have a target area and a target player—someone tall and a good header of the ball. The target player will be asked to flick the ball behind him for his teammates to get to (commonly called the second ball). In most cases, the target area is the near post, with the target player coming to the target area at speed, but late. The target player and the ball should arrive at the same time. The target player does not want to be caught standing in the target area, because he will be easier to mark and will lose height in his jump.

Illus. 247

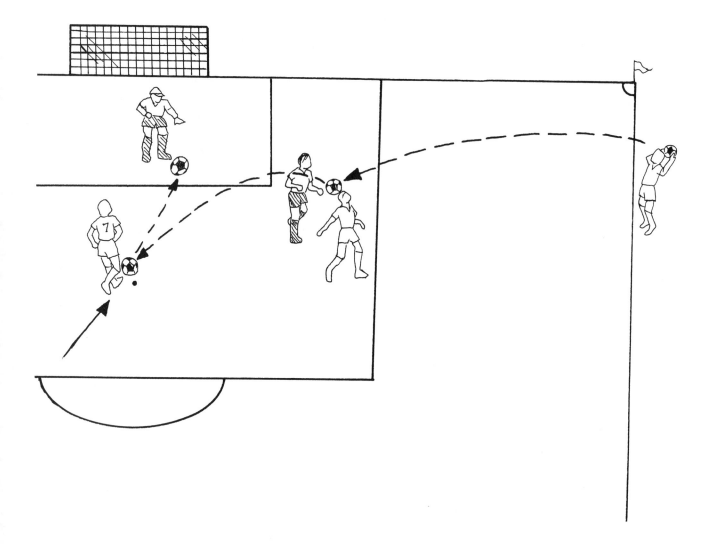

Direct Free Kicks

A direct free kick is awarded when one of the nine major fouls have been committed. On a direct free kick, the attacking team can score a goal directly without having the ball touch any players before entering the goal. Direct free kicks are broken down into two different types: direct shots that can be taken, and direct shots that cannot be taken.

Illus. 248. When the attacking team has a direct free kick in direct shooting distance of the goal, they should try to beat the wall with a direct shot on goal. Many goals are scored this way on rebounds off defenders, the goalkeeper, goal post, and the crossbar. These shots must be followed up, but these second chances will not occur if the direct shot does not hit the target. The first emphasis is hitting the target with the direct shot.

Illus. 248

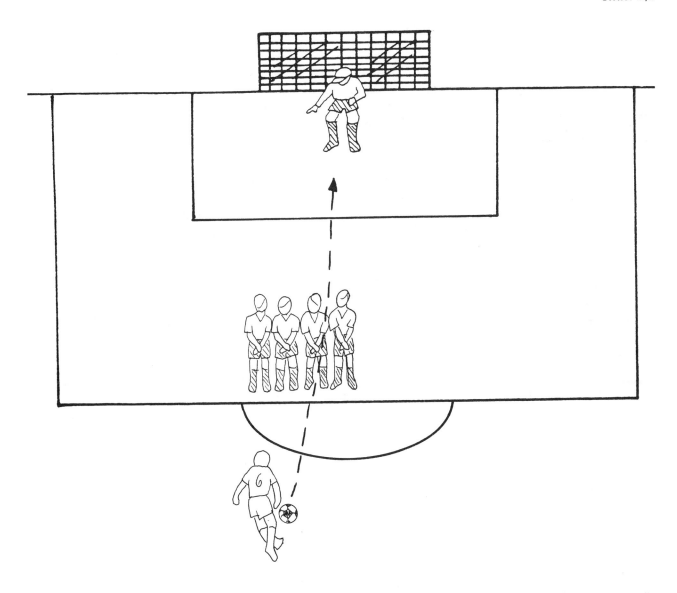

Indirect Free Kicks

An indirect free kick is one where the ball must be touched twice before it can enter the goal. Because of this a direct shot on goal should be taken on the second touch by the second player, and there are ways that the wall can be beaten by the first touch (the pass).

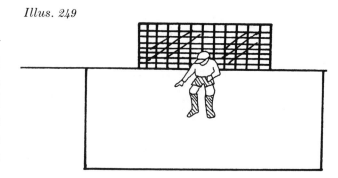

Illus. 249

Illus. 249. The wall can be beaten by passing the ball square in front of it. Playing the ball square and inside will uncover the space and the part of the goal which the wall is covering. The shot should be driven back into this open space.

Illus. 250. Another way to beat the wall is to play the ball into space alongside of the wall for a cross into the danger area, or better, a direct shot on goal.

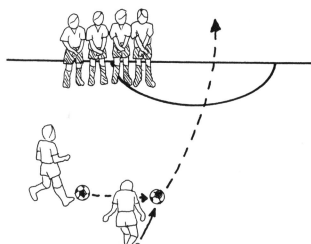

Illus. 250

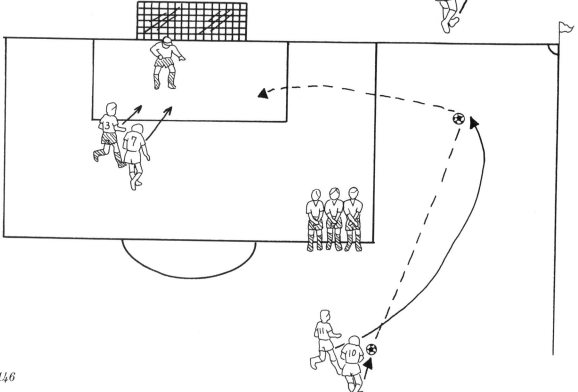

146

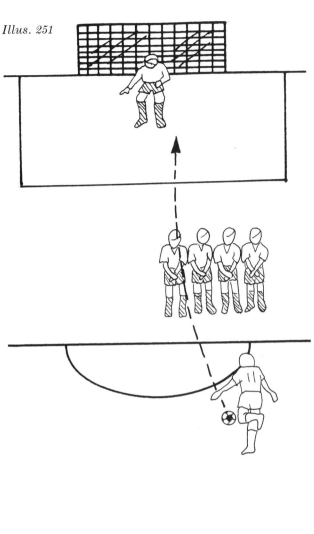

Illus. 251

Illus. 251. The third way is to play the ball over the wall into the space behind the wall, where it can meet an attacking player.

Inside The Penalty Box

Illus. 252. If a free kick is given inside the penalty box, the attacker is probably going to have to beat all eleven defending players in order to score, and if the free kick is awarded less than 10 yards from the goal, the defending team will build a human wall along the goal line. To beat this human wall, there are several points to remember.

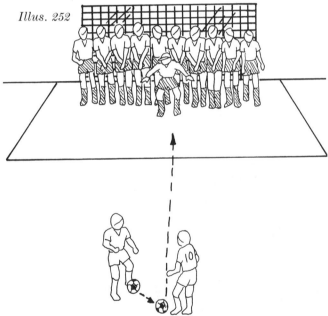

Illus. 252

Coaching Points

• Keep your attacking players calm.
• If the ball is at a narrow angle, the first touch should widen the angle to the inside of the goal. Play this first touch back away from goal and not square. With the ball being played to the inside to widen the angle, there will also be more target at which to shoot.
• If the kick is more centralized, play the first touch back away from goal. This gives the shooter more time and space. A ball coming to the shooter is much easier to strike and to get the ball in the air than a ball which runs across the face of the shooter.
• Aim high and away from the goalkeeper.

Corner Kicks

Illus. 253. When planning for attacking cor- ner kicks, take two important points into con- sideration:

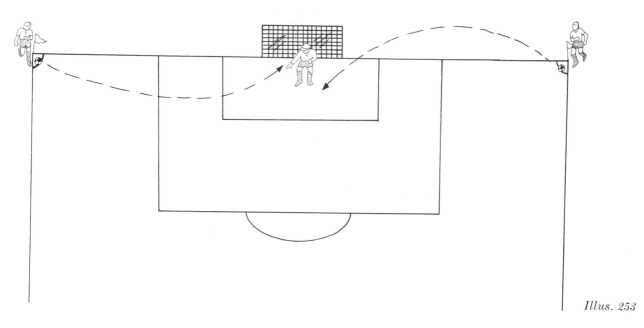

Illus. 253

The Inswinging Corner Kick

The inswinging corner kick has advantages and disadvantages.

Illus. 254. One advantage is it applies great pressure to the defending team and goal-keeper. In most cases, the inswinging corner kick is driven, thus making it very difficult for the goalkeeper to handle, and hard for the defending team to clear. Also, with the ball bending in towards the goal, there is always the possibility of the ball going straight into the goal from the corner kick.

Illus. 255. With the inswinging corner kick, the ball can be driven to the near post. This will force the goalkeeper to make a decision, either to stay and have his defensive team-mates clear the ball, or to come at speed to the near post to catch or clear the ball, again applying great pressure to the defending team.

Illus. 256. If a team is going to play inswinging corner kicks, it is recommended that an attacking player be positioned in front of the goalkeeper to block his vision and path to the ball.

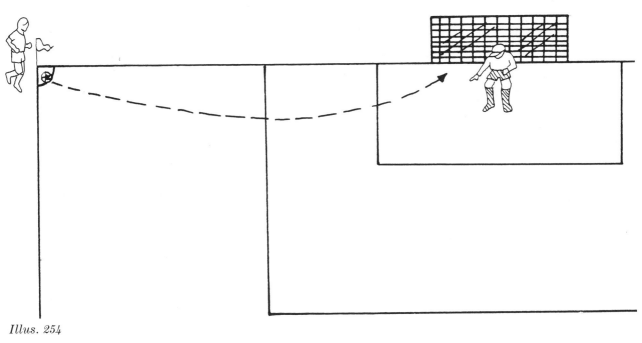

Illus. 254

Illus. 255

Illus. 256

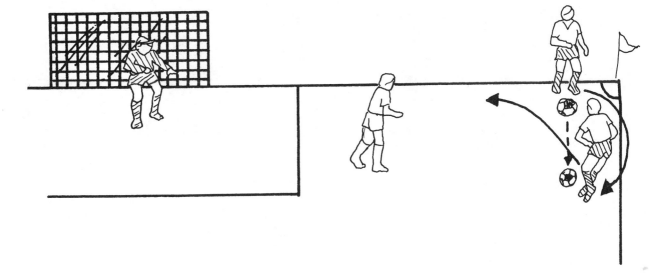

Illus. 257. With the ball bending in towards the goal, the attacking team may only have to redirect the ball for it to go in.

Illus. 258. With the inswinging corner kick, there is always the possibility of the ball going in because of a missed defensive clearance.

Illus. 258

Illus. 259

Illus. 260

Illus. 259. One disadvantage to the inswinging corner kick is it puts pressure on the server to be very accurate with the service. Because of this requirement, the ball will often go out of play at the near post or even over the crossbar.

Illus. 260. Another disadvantage is when the ball is played in towards the goal, the path of the ball makes it easier for it to be cleared.

The Outswinging Corner Kick

Illus. 261. This set piece has many advantages. For one, this type of service can fool the goalkeeper. He picks up the line of the ball; then starts to commit himself, only to have the ball bend away from him at the last moment.

Illus. 261

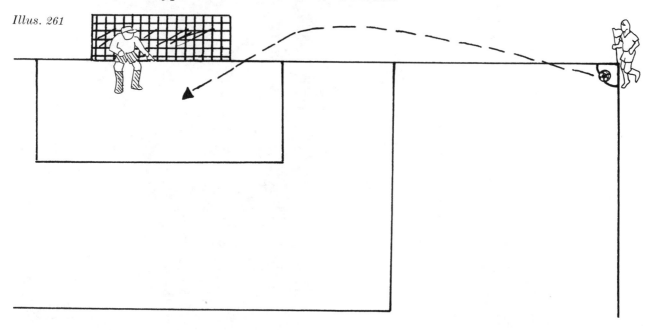

Illus. 262. When the ball is bending away from the goal, it is also bending into the path of the oncoming attacking players. This makes it easier for the attacking players to strike the ball at goal. The attacking player can also use the pace of the ball in his favor to gain power for the shot on goal.

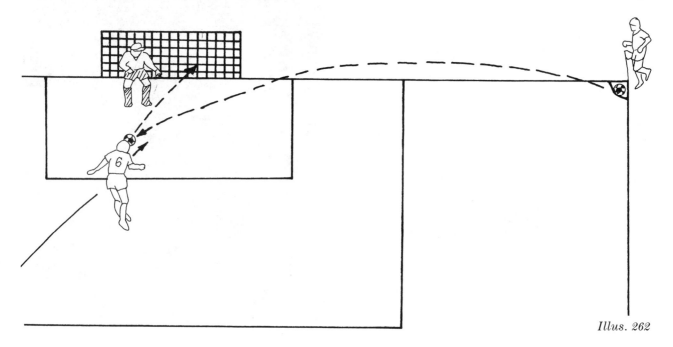

Illus. 262

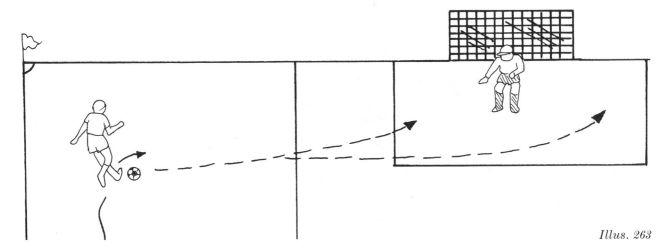

Illus. 263. The server has the option of playing the ball to either the near or far post, thus giving the attacking team two target areas.

Illus. 264. However, it has two disadvantages. The first is any immediate chance of the ball going straight into the goal is lost, as is the possibility of the ball hitting a defending player and going in. Since the goalkeeper may not have to handle any crosser, it eliminates any chance of the goalkeeper making a mistake.

Illus. 264

Illus. 265

Illus. 265. Another disadvantage is that it is harder for the defending team to clear the ball from the danger area. The path of the ball is bending away from the defending players, making it harder to get to the ball.

Short Corner

The attacking team will use a short corner either to have the serve taken closer to the goal and at a wider angle; or to get a shot on goal. When using a short corner, remember that the 10-yard rule will allow the attacking team to place two players on the ball and keep any defending players away from the ball until it has been played. After the attacking player plays the ball to his teammates, he must then get out of an offside position and behind the ball.

Illus. 266. The attacking player who has possession of the ball must attack the defensive by going down the line towards the goal.

Illus. 267. When the defending team reacts and challenges the attacking player with the ball, it draws defending players out of the danger area. This creates time and space for the attacking team. When the attacking player is challenged, he will attempt to pass the ball back to the attacking player who originally played the ball. This player will now look to serve the ball. On a narrow field the short corner can be used to get a shot on goal.

If a corner is on the right, the attacking side will try to have a left-footed player serve or shoot the ball. The opposite applies on the left attacking side: have a right-footed player serve or shoot the ball.

154

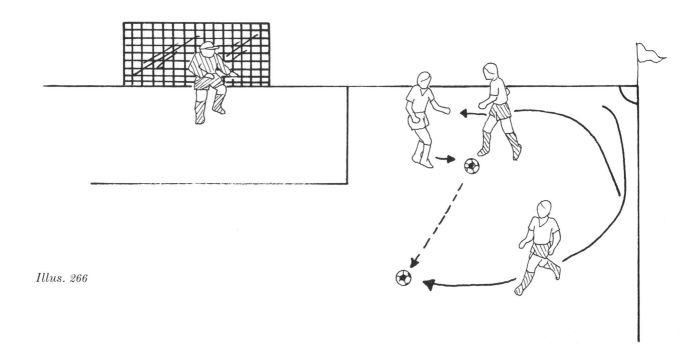

Illus. 266

Illus. 267

155

Index